To Adi,

Jawatta Road

Love

Nicola

xxx

Jawatta Road

A Ceylon Childhood

Judy Shattock

Matador
9 Priory Business Park,
Wistow Road, Kibworth Beauchamp,
Leicestershire. LE8 0RX
Tel: 0116 279 2299
Email: books@troubador.co.uk
Web: www.troubador.co.uk/matador
Twitter: @matadorbooks

ISBN 978 1788037 358

British Library Cataloguing in Publication Data.
A catalogue record for this book is available from the British Library.

Printed and bound by CPI Group (UK) Ltd, Croydon, CR0 4YY
Typeset in 11pt Aldine401 BT by Troubador Publishing Ltd, Leicester, UK

Matador is an imprint of Troubador Publishing Ltd

MIX
Paper from
responsible sources
FSC® C013604

For my daughters: Katya, Alexie and Gabriella, with love.

'You are the bow from which your children as living arrows are sent forth'

The Prophet, Kahlil Gibran

Chapter 1

A Chance Encounter

As he hurried down the hill from his home in Great Austins, Gary had no idea what an auspicious day it would be. He was on his way to Farnham station, already late for the 7.25 to London. Mentally, he checked he had everything in his briefcase – gas mask, files, notes, sandwich, and most importantly, the metal tin holding his inhaler. It was April 1940, and medical knowledge for those with asthma was limited. He had to put this glass contraption in his mouth, squeeze the rubber bulb and breathe in a spray of medication to relax his chest. He had had a bad night, shortness of breath making sleep impossible. Glancing at his watch he realised he would now miss his train. No point hurrying, he would have to catch the next, slow, frequently stopping train. He would make Throckmorton Road, where he was training to be a tea taster, shortly after 9.30.

Queuing for his paper he caught sight of his reflection in the glass. Smoothing his unruly thick black curly hair, noting his lean frame in a smart grey suit, he thought of his older brother Bobby, who had lent it to him. "Here, Edgar, use my suit, now you have that fancy job in the city. Since joining the Air Force I am in and out of planes, I hardly use it." The Germans were bombing Belgium,

- 1 -

getting nearer England; flocks of young men had signed up and were being trained to fly. Henry, Gary's eldest brother, was already a commander in the Navy. Frustrated by his poor health, Gary had joined the Home Guard, thinking at least he would do something for his country.

Clambering onto the crowded, smoky train, he found a seat, feeling the lurch as the train moved away from Farnham, tired and angry with himself for being late. He dozed. Hearing brakes squeal, he braced himself for the stop. As the doors opened with a blast of cold air, he looked out of the grimy window. Ash Vale. The doors slammed shut, the whistle blew.

And there she stood. He blinked, stared. She held onto the luggage rack as the train jerked away, her trim figure swaying with the movement, a small hat perched on her dark hair, searching for a place to sit. He jumped up, tiredness forgotten. "Please, please, sit here." His words came out with a croak – his throat was dry, his heart thumping. Her blue-grey eyes, framed with dark lashes, smiled at him. Her lips were red. She was beautiful.

"Thank you," she said, as she moved to sit, brushing past him. He caught a whiff of her perfume.

This is how I imagined my father met the love of his life, my mother, Jean.

Chapter 2

Colonial Past

We all know families can be difficult. Jean's parents, the Barrington-Gateses, and Gary's family, the Shattocks, could not have been more different. Seventy years ago these differences made it hard for a young couple in love. Their chance encounter was to lead to eternal family conflict.

Gary's family had a long history in Ceylon, where he had spent the early years of his life. I have some old sepia-coloured photos taken of his mother, Mabel, at her wedding in 1901. The family lived near Ratnapura, in the district of Sabaragamuwa, a gem mining area in the southern part of the island, where my great-grandfather, Evan Byrde, worked for the government as a district judge. The wedding party is formally arranged down the steps of the veranda of a tea estate bungalow, potted plants and ferns softening the picture. My severe-looking great-grandmother is seated, wearing a full-length, tight-waisted, sprigged muslin dress, a black toque trimmed with dark red and pink roses on her head, dressed in the very height of fashion. Evan is next to her. Mabel, his favourite daughter, stands proudly next to her new husband, the dark-haired Ernest Shattock, who worked in Lee Hedges, one of the trading houses in Colombo.

My father told me very little about his past. "My mother Mabel was so beautiful that she turned many heads at the Colombo races. When she took the train to Colombo, after her marriage, on every station platform stood a broken-hearted suitor, waving her goodbye!"

Mabel and Ernest went to live in Colombo and, over a period of fifteen years, had six children – Henry, Violet, Joan, Bobby, a daughter who died in infancy, and later, my father, Edgar Charles Evan. These children were raised partly in Ceylon and then in England, where they were sent, at a very early age, to boarding school. Ernest died aged fifty-four, of Bright's disease, at their English home in Churt, Surrey, where he is buried in the churchyard, his old lichen-covered headstone standing crooked with age.

Mabel, obviously still a stylish beauty despite having had six children, then married Charles Burns, who also worked as a trader in the Lee Hedges office. Ernest and Charles must have been good friends. History does not relate, but they worked for the same company and the families would have known each other well, in the small ex-patriot Colombo community.

Mabel returned to Ceylon with Charles to live the grand lifestyle, but this time upcountry in Doone Lodge, near Nuwara Eliya, where they employed a retinue of servants, enabling them to have many house guests and parties. I have photos of Joan, Bobby and Gary on the tennis court or on horseback or having picnics with their cousins and friends, always with one of Bobby's beautiful cars in the picture. This was during the Depression when vast sums of money were lost overnight.

Edgar, or Gary, as he was affectionately called, was out there on holiday, enjoying his freedom from Lancing College in England, when he returned home from a bicycling adventure one day to find his stepfather had blown his brains out. My aunt Violet used to say to me, "There was a big scandal but no one ever talked about it. It was a terrible business."

Chapter 3

A Family from Norfolk

By contrast, my mother, Jean, had never set foot outside England. She had been at school in Farnham, taking prizes for swimming and diving. Edith Annie Tofts, Jean's mother, was a highly intelligent farmer's daughter from Norfolk. Adept at cooking, well versed in country life, an accomplished musician, and sporty, Annie had met Sydney Barrington-Gates, always known as Barry, whilst playing tennis in Cambridge. I have often wondered whether the fact that Annie was ten years older than Barry raised eyebrows in those days. She must have been a dynamic force to have captured the heart of this young, handsome, somewhat silent scholar.

Barry had such a severe stammer that he could barely communicate. To listen to him trying to talk was painful; each word came out after hesitations and long pauses. It affected him badly all his life. An athletic, sensitive child, he was brought up near Bury St Edmunds, until his Father moved the family to Norwich, when he became manager of Barclays Bank. At the City of Norwich school, Barry's genius was nurtured by his maths master, enabling him to win a mathematics scholarship to Corpus Christi, Cambridge. Life opened up and he gained a First, finally being recruited by the chief engineer at the Royal

Aircraft factory, which later became the Royal Aircraft Establishment at Farnborough.

In his day, Barry was considered to be the world's leading expert on aircraft stability, advising American aircraft designers Boeing, Douglas, Northrop and Lockheed, on all stability and control aspects of aircraft designs. In 1942, he travelled with H.B. Thomas as a spokesperson. They made an impressive duo; the Americans were riveted.

His disability affected his personality. He was unable to enter into lively discussions or communicate easily at the simplest level. Instead, he was forced to write notes. He appeared taciturn and withdrawn, as indeed he was, living inside his head, enclosed in his own world. Every day he walked down the road, climbing the wooden stairs of Ash Vale station to collect his copy of the *Manchester Guardian*. He was a staunch socialist.

You can imagine the effect this had on Anne, Jean and Michael, growing up with a silent father, wreathed in pipe smoke, shut up in his book-lined study, reviewing travel books, correcting Cambridge maths papers, writing numerous academic papers, or simply gazing out through the windows onto his beloved garden.

Jean was headstrong, clever, moody and very attractive. She was training to be a beautician in London, when war broke out.

Years later, Uncle Michael was surprisingly informative about the family. A strange man who hardly spoke, extremely dark-haired, with a slight stutter like his father, who lived at home in the dark, top, back bedroom, the door of which was opposite the door to Granny's bedroom.

When he was out at work and Granny downstairs, I used to peer around his bedroom door, curious to find out something about my uncle, who was also my godfather. It was bare save for a dark blue bedspread, dark curtains and a small rug on wooden floorboards. A high chest of drawers held a hairbrush. It smelt male. I never went far in. Somehow it was frightening.

Each year, on my birthday, a card arrived with a ten-pound note neatly folded inside. And always, written at an angle, on the bottom-left corner of the card in his distinctive, cramped style, were the few words, "With love from Uncle Michael." He never forgot.

He was always bitter about his father, accusing him of having sent him to a repressive boarding school. He appeared to have hated him, intimating that he took walking holidays with other women, never having the time of day for him. He was very aware of his father's girlfriends, and, although he loved his sister, he may well have been jealous of the ease in which she collected boyfriends, quickly casting them off, the infidelity going both ways.

"Jean could twist Father around her little finger. She managed to persuade him to put a phone in the house. You remember the cupboard under the stairs? There was a small space there, between the wall and the cupboard door! That was where Father put this modern contraption. She would sit for hours, beside the stairs, night after night, talking to her boyfriends. Then she would take the best offer! And off she went!"

I remember that place well. Behind the stairs at Firgrove was a small table, on which was an old-fashioned black telephone with a stool beside it, and on the wall hung Granny's list of phone numbers. She would shuffle slowly using her sticks to walk. Sometimes she leaned on the trolley to help her along the corridor. Both her hips were stiff and painful, her movement severely limited with arthritis. Walking down the narrow passageway, turning around at the end, she eased herself onto the hard stool, before using the phone. The phone must have been my grandmother's lifeline, as well as my mother's.

Amongst my papers is a long, stern letter written by my grandfather to Jean on the subject of men, suggesting she had little taste, accusing her of being promiscuous, of playing sex games, of having too many boyfriends, and advising her to think of other people's feelings. It makes fascinating reading, not only because Grandpa wrote fluently with a stylish script, but also that this document, written on Royal Aircraft Establishment note paper, still exists. The subject matter shocked me. It still makes uncomfortable reading, all these years later. It's the only letter I have of hers. I wonder why she kept it.

Possibly it had the desired effect. Jean married Gary.

This proposed marriage caused some consternation in Gary's family, as Jean's family, the Barrington-Gateses, were staunch socialists, whereas the Shattocks were extremely conservative. In those long ago days of 1941, political affiliations were nearly as important as religion. You can imagine the conversations that went on: "Who is this girl that Edgar wants to marry?" "He seems to have met her on a train!" "Does he realise how very different her family are?" Or possibly, "Jean is very attractive. She goes to London every day to work! Have you heard about her father? A real boffin! Does Edgar really know what he is doing?"

Perhaps Jean's parents were relieved she had made her choice at last – the string of boyfriends would stop, the telephone would be used less.

Chapter 4

War Years

Jean and Gary married; their wedding reception was held at The Hog's Back Hotel, which used to be a stylish location and, conveniently, was situated halfway between Farnham and Ash Vale. Looking at the photographs now, seventy years later, they make a handsome couple. Posing on the steps at Firgrove, hand in hand, both are happy and smiling, looking expectant. It gives me such a warm feeling. My father wears a smart double-breasted, high-collar pinstriped suit, with a carnation in his buttonhole and well-polished shoes. Jean has a fitted coat with small brass buttons down the front, a cheeky hat perched to the side of her head, a spray of lily of the valley pinned on her corsage. She is holding a horseshoe for luck.

They went to live at The Sheiling, in Hamble, on Southampton water. Gary's severe asthma precluded active service so he worked at the nearby Folland Aircraft factory, which was producing much-needed ammunition for the war. Starting work as a fitter, he finally became personal assistant to the managing director. Nicola was born in May 1942 and I arrived two years later.

All did not go smoothly. It was wartime, there was food rationing, Jean was some distance from her parents, and with two small children, Nicola in particular was causing her problems. Party time was over.

Or perhaps not.

Jean ran off with a photographer, Jack Wyatt, who she had met in Hamble. Nicola and I must have gone with her because the affair carried on for quite a while. My father returned to Colombo to work, leaving us behind. This has never been mentioned, naturally, but families often let things slip. Painful memories were all buried deep under the carpet. Jean's departure must have been a real body blow to Gary's pride. His constant asthma attacks which were the reason that he never had been able to complete his schooling or, indeed, his degree course at Cambridge, had left him with something of a complex. He was a complicated personality, a true Piscean, wanting to swim in two directions at once. On one hand, although he was a stickler for doing everything the correct way, he was also generous, thoughtful, loving, full of *joie de vivre*, crazily turning up the volume of his beloved jazz music, then suddenly, with almost no warning, he would become moody, anxious, introverted.

No one can imagine how Gary must have felt to live with a constantly tight chest and shortness of breath, fearful in the knowledge that the next sudden attack may be the end. He certainly was hard to live with. I never knew what sort of mood he would be in and consequently behaved well so as not to anger him.

There are some particularly stunning pictures of me and Nicola as small children which hung on the wall of the long, dark, upstairs corridor of Firgrove. When I grew older and Nicola, by then, was not with me, I would often stand in the gloomy light just outside the bathroom, staring at these photos, wondering about my mother, whether she loved us, where we were living when they were taken, whether our life may have been quite different. I have always assumed that Jack took these pictures. Nicola, her fine hair in plaits, held back with slides, smiles straight at the camera. I, on the other hand, am looking at someone to the side, hair all over my baby face, podgy little fingers playing with a toy, aged about two and a half, already getting used to being without my father.

Chapter 5

Ceylon

Gary, in the meantime, had joined the same trading company in Colombo in which his father and stepfather had worked. This company had been started in the 1800s by Mr Lee and Mr Hedges, who must have discovered a gap in the market for graphite. These mines in Ceylon produced a high-quality, much sought-after graphite. The company exported this commodity as well as timber, and acted as an agency house for some of the earliest tea and rubber growing ventures. Later, the company expanded by importing fertiliser, liquor and chemicals, and became agents for shipping, airlines and insurance companies.

My parents must have become reconciled, as in 1947 the four of us boarded one of the Bibby Liners bound for Colombo. Jean would have felt so many emotions – excitement, fear, apprehension. Sailing off into the unknown with a husband with whom she may not have wanted to live, taking us and her away from all that was secure for her. Perhaps she had been given another talking to by her father. I shall never know. Unusually, as he was not known for strong emotional displays, my grandfather travelled to Southampton to say farewell to his favourite daughter. Perhaps he had had a strong sense of foreboding.

Jean would have found life on board for the four-week boat journey via Port Said, the Suez Canal, Port Sudan and Aden, exciting and vibrant; unlike anything she had ever done before. She was a party girl and loved the bright lights and having fun. On board, ship life was comfortable, with days structured around mealtimes. These were announced by a gong, which stood at the bottom of the stairs close to the dining room. It had a large round brass face and took some beating. The steward used a long wooden hammer, the end of which was covered with padded leather. The reverberations could be heard echoing throughout the ship.

Once through the Bay of Biscay, notorious for its appalling rough seas, when the ship rolled frighteningly from side to side and many passengers had to retire to their cabins, the crew arranged games of deck quoits, badminton and quizzes. A raised pool made from canvas which was filled with sea water when the weather became warmer, formed the focal point for families with young children. Deck chairs were arranged close by. Friendships would have been made; old friendships renewed. Jean would have met young people returning to the east after the war, some for the first time like her, others with children, already old colonial hands returning from home leave. Nicola and I would have made friends, running around the decks, jumping into the pool, splashing, shouting, jumping out to be wrapped in thick towels, quite safe.

Jean and Gary would have dressed up for dinner; there would have been music and dancing, visits to the bridge, drinks with the captain, walks around the gently rolling decks at night under a vast canopy of stars with the phosphorescence in the sea leaving a white luminous trail behind the stern.

Finally, the smell of earth wafted on the breeze as we all crowded on deck, anxious for the first glimpse of land. We had been at sea for too long and the atmosphere on board was full of excitement and anticipation. We moored in Colombo harbour where customs and immigration officials, all smartly dressed in white shirts and shorts, arrived alongside by boat. Once they had clambered up on board to check our papers we were free to disembark. We had to wait for the harbour boats which ferried us through the busy water to the main quay, where we climbed up the steps to the baggage hall. Now we had to wait for our trunks, then file out through the ornate entrance into the main road. What a different life lay ahead for all of us.

Jean, Nicola and I had never seen dark-skinned porters. They were shouting to each other, chewing beetle nut, spitting streams of red liquid onto the ground, smiling at us. The new arrivals were standing, looking pale and bewildered, staring at them; with their red-stained teeth, dressed in dhoti and vest. The heat would have been oppressive: the fish harbour, stinking, close by; flies swarming over dirt on the narrow roads; crowds milling around, stepping over pools of foetid water; bare-footed men carrying heavy loads; bullock carts piled high with bananas, lengths of wood, boxes; the owner, sitting behind his bullock, kicking his rear end with his toe to urge him on.

We were met by the company's representative, who would have smoothed over the formalities of arrival, beckoning for the car and driver to take us to the hotel.

Chapter 6

Galle Face Hotel

Life was one big adventure for us. We arrived at the Galle Face Hotel, positioned right on the seafront, where we were given a suite of rooms until a house was sorted out for us. Humidity was intense, spray rising from incessant waves beating against the promenade, filling our nostrils with that particular salty smell. This big, white, colonnaded hotel, standing on the main road to Galle, the old capital, was a short distance from the parliament building, the Anglican church and smart shops.

Imposing steps led up to a grand entrance, where the doorman, dressed in white sarong and jacket, wearing the traditional tortoiseshell comb in his hair, salaamed and greeted every person entering this oasis of colonial style. Highly polished brass door handles were evident, along with shining wooden floorboards and ostentatious vases filled with red anthuriums. Brown wood ceiling fans whirred endlessly, keeping us cool. Smartly dressed waiters hovered in doorways, speedily arriving at our rooms when we rang the bell. Nothing appeared to be too much effort; all the staff made a fuss of us both, bringing the smallest item which would make us more comfortable.

It was a sybaritic lifestyle, especially as we had just

arrived from austere, post-war England, where food rationing had been enforced, men were out of work and families who had lost loved ones and had been separated from each other were learning to live again. Jean did not have to shop for food, cook or wash up, clean her rooms or make the beds. Food was plentiful. Prawns, crabs and other fish straight from the ocean; fruits which we had never tasted before – mangoes, papaya, bananas, pineapple, limes, lychees, rambutans, mangosteens – arrived on the table as a matter of course. Spicy curries were flavoured with coconut milk. One curry meal alone would contain at least five dishes, accompanied by a large steaming bowl of rice and small dishes of chutney and spicy relishes.

A formal garden between the back of the hotel and the sea provided a protected space, a large garden where we could play while our ayah watched us. Jean loved the large saltwater pool, where loungers were arranged directly overlooking the ocean, and she swam daily. She must have revelled in her freedom with endless hot sun and fresh white towels which were handed to her as she went to dry in the changing room. Afterwards, we would join her for tea, our ayah waiting respectfully in the background until she was needed again.

We took our afternoon walks along the seafront where a wide esplanade, constructed six feet above the sandy beach, stretched into the distance towards the harbour and parliament buildings. In the cool of the evenings, crowds gathered in family groups on the adjacent Galle Face Green. Some walked, gently chattering, the women dressed in brightly coloured saris, children running in and out of the crowds. The kite seller was much in demand;

fathers taught their sons the art of catching the breeze, while teenagers staged competitions with their brightly coloured paper kites, which swooped and soared above the crowd. Spicy peanuts wrapped in newspaper cones were sold from small handcarts whose kerosene lamps were beginning to twinkle in the dusk.

Chapter 7

Beach Road

By this time Nicola was five and causing concern as her fitting episodes were becoming more regular. Nicola had been born at my grandparents' house in Ash Vale, in May 1942. In those days babies were routinely delivered at home. The local doctor had been called; my mother was in distress as the baby was slow in arriving. Finally, he'd had to use forceps, old-fashioned metal contraptions. These had caused the damage, so I was told many years later. "Nicola cried non-stop for six weeks after she was born," my father said. Poor Nicola, how she must have suffered. She must have been in terrible pain, with pressure on her brain. Very little was understood about brain damage seventy years ago. It must have been hard for them all, constantly worrying about her, never quite knowing when she would have a fit, as they were called in those days. People who had fits were considered to be mad. Doctors were not much help as they didn't know what to suggest for the epileptic seizures – *petit mal*, which is what they are called today.

Nicola came out of these fits quite quickly, but always needed someone close by to watch her. Often we had to call the doctor. Ayah would have been an invaluable help, caring for me while all the attention was on my sister. Nicola was always slow to complete physical activities. She needed help to dress, was slow to learn to read, and had a faraway look in her eyes.

Beside me I have three photos, taken around this time, of my mother on a beach. There she is, walking out of the waves, laughing. She is wide-hipped with a slim waist, her one-piece costume showing off strong, shapely legs. And now, behind her while she is standing, her head bent talking to Nicola and me, who are both sitting on the sand, is a forest of graceful palm trees lining the shore. The sand looks smooth and firm, clean and uncluttered; our family group is sitting on the shining wetness where the retreating sea has left its mark. Jean's friend – I never knew her name – is close by, leaning back on her hands, also smiling, while her young son runs in from the sea.

In the second picture Jean is sitting in the shallow water, her dark hair and shoulders framed by the endless sky and gently breaking waves, holding me over her knees, her hands under my bottom, while I am clutching her arms, looking slightly fearful. She is talking quietly in my ear, encouraging me to kick my legs in the warm tropical water. My mother looks young, strong and capable on this sunny morning long ago. And here she is again, sitting in between Nicola and me, just on the gentle wave's break, all three of us smiling at the camera. I wish I could go back to that time with her, recapture those moments when she held me in the water. Even now, my heart breaks to look at us all so happy there; one moment, captured forever.

That beach is south of Colombo, close to Mount Lavinia Hotel. The turn-off from the main road out of

Colombo towards Galle, which used to be the old capital, was extremely narrow and easy to miss. It was marked 'Beach Road'. Our excitement would heighten as we started to bump down the rutted lane, which sloping steeply downhill was bounded on both sides by high walls plastered with old, faded handbills. There was anticipation of who would be the first to shout "the sea!" which meant that soon we could climb out of the hot car, and our sticky bodies would feel free. Finally, the road gave way to open sand where my father parked the car under the shade of a convenient palm. Carrying a beach bag and towels, our parents held our hands while we carefully crossed the railway line before reaching the wide expanse of beach with its sparkling turquoise-blue sea stretching faraway to the horizon. We had our special spot where we always left our clothes, under the shade of another palm. This one leaned at a wicked angle; we always hoped that spot would be free.

Once our life had settled into a routine, we went to the beach every Sunday morning before returning home sandy, covered with a film of dried, slightly crusty salt, tired but happy for a late lunch.

Chapter 8

A Glass of Water

Life was fun and happy. I was too young to realise our idyllic family days were limited.

All expatriate families knew they had to be extremely cautious about their drinking water. It had been drilled into them from the moment they stepped off the boat: "Do not drink water from the tap." In our house, water had to be boiled for ten minutes, before being poured into the heavy stone filter which stood on a wooden table in the pantry. A small tap at the bottom of the filter let out the pure liquid, drip by drip. Cleaned whisky or gin bottles, standing like sentries below the filter, collected these precious drops. These frosted bottles lay motionless, side by side, cooling in the ice box. Only then was water declared fit for drinking.

This was a job for the podian, a young Singhalese boy who was learning kitchen and household skills along with all the whims of foreigners. Tap water was forbidden to be used, even for teeth cleaning. A carafe of filtered water was put on the bathroom shelf especially for this purpose. Every household did this. It tasted horrible: warm and flat. Swilling it around my mouth, quickly spitting every last drop into the basin, I wiped the moisture away briskly on the hand towel.

We were not allowed drinks outside the house with ice in. "You don't know whether they have boiled the water before making the ice," my father always said. "Don't drink from the bottle; there will be dirt around the edge. Use a glass; make sure it has been wiped dry. Or use a straw." He frightened me with his strictness, piercing me with a stern look from under his bushy eyebrows. Ice cream from outside our home, food from wayside stalls which smelt so enticing, or cups of tea from street vendors, were all forbidden. Now I know why.

Jean – headstrong, independent, obstinate – probably did not take too kindly to being told what to do in this strange country. Perhaps she had not heard of dysentery, or even worse, typhoid fever. We still don't know why she did it. Everything started with a glass of water, according to my father – "Jean insisted on drinking tap water." I don't know whether my father made it up, just being Edgarish. It was always hard to know whether he was serious or not. I never even thought to ask him a direct question. Jean certainly was not careful; she thought she knew best, she didn't listen to other people. Perhaps she didn't care. Perhaps she was extremely unhappy, so far from all that she had known in her life. Perhaps she was having such a marvellous time she didn't understand the consequences of something as simple as drinking tap water. When, during all one's life, clean water has always been on hand, flowing so generously, when one is thirsty it seems so simple to take a glass and fill it from the tap. Looking back, I still have doubts as to whether my mother drank the water on purpose.

Towards the end of January 1949, suddenly a high

fever hit her. She was taken to the private Fraser Nursing Home in Cinnamon Gardens, close to where we lived. She was seriously ill. It would have come upon her suddenly, without warning. She was shivering, her tanned skin boiling hot, her dark hair wet with perspiration. Jean was in a delirium, incoherent. "Mummy is not well, she is in hospital." We waited anxiously at home, our ayah doing her best to distract us. When it seemed opportune, Nicola and I were taken to visit her.

I remember standing beside her high metal bed, scared, frightened, not understanding why my mother was lying there, so still. Nicola and I stood close together, holding each other's hands, not knowing what to do. The room was cool and dim with no colours inside. Greys, white, a dark polished floor, the shutters closed against the sun, a smell of antiseptic, a sense of hush, only the fan slowly whirring. The regular click-click of the vanes, strangely comforting. There was a frame over her, on which the nurses had put a sheet in an effort to keep her cool, so the air could circulate around her fevered body.

She opened her eyes and saw us, speaking to us quietly and gently, asking us what we had been doing at home. Those were to be her last words to us. She came out of her delirium for that brief moment in time. The nurses were amazed, said it was a miracle. We were taken home. We never saw her again. There was no medicine available for typhoid fever in Colombo at that time. It had been sent for from America, urgently, but arrived too late. She died the very next day and was quickly buried in the Anglican section of the Kanatte cemetery at the end of Bullers Road, about a mile from where we lived.

Chapter 9

Back to England

I was now four, Nicola was six. We must have been dazed, confused, wondering what on earth was happening to us. We had only just become settled in Colombo, used to the heat, the different lifestyle. We had a garden full of flowering trees, the sun was always shining. Living in a large, airy house we had become used to our dark-skinned ayah who cared for us during the day. My father was left with no option but to send us back to England by boat. This would be another four-week journey, in the care of friends who were returning on leave. In the course of our young lives, we had already been moved from place to place by my mother and now, because of her sudden death, we were on the move again.

My grandparents must have been devastated; my grandfather seemed to have a sixth sense that he would never see his daughter again. I don't think they ever forgave my father.

We went to live with my grandparents at Firgrove. Perhaps they found it too difficult caring for us, two small lost girls, homesick and missing our mother and father. Nicola had special needs and it was winter time, the evenings dark. We needed to go to school, to have some structure in our day. We must have been a constant reminder of their lost, beloved, lively daughter Jean. We didn't stay with them for long. Grandpa, who had unusual ideas about education, decided to send us to a 'progressive' boarding school on the Hog's Back, close to them in Surrey.

Once again our clothes were packed up, and Nicola and I were bundled off into the unknown. A beamed gatehouse, which was built just off the A31, close to the start of the high-ridged Hog's Back Road, stood at the entrance of a long gravelled drive leading up a hill. Here stood an imposing house – our future school. The entrance gates were kept closed. We were cut off from the world.

I slept in a dormitory where my bed had a mattress comprising of three cushions. Each night, waking up with my bedding awry, cushions on the floor, I felt lost, cold. Everyone else was asleep. I was extremely uncomfortable and lonely. Putting the cushions straight, I went back to sleep, only to wake again, anxious. I remember gazing at the stars during those wakeful nights, wondering about my mother, thinking about my father, so far away. I never told anyone. We just had to fit in with life in that strange place.

One day we were all given the task of digging a deep hole to construct a pool in the bottom of the garden. We had to carry large rocks, which had been dug up, to a nearby pile. It was hard work for small children. We seemed to be there all morning. One boy constantly taunted me. I had had enough. I was miserable. With all my frustrated rage, I dropped a particularly heavy stone on his foot. I'm sure it bled. I got into serious trouble and was locked in my dormitory. No one bothered to ask why

I had dropped the stone. I cried my heart out. It was a long day and it was evening time before I was let out.

There was nobody who seemed to care about us; no one gave us a hug. On Sundays we were given sweets, but they were thrown over the floor so we had to run to collect them. Perhaps the school's policy was to teach us that we had to fight for what we wanted in life. I wish I had asked my grandparents when I grew up why they chose that place for us.

Once a week we did go horse riding at the Hog's Back Riding School, along heathland and through beautiful, meandering Surrey paths. This was the highlight of our life, Nicola and I, trotting along, side by side, on ponies far too big for us. Our other outing was being allowed to walk the mile up the hill to the nearest shop in crocodile formation, rattling sticks along the wooden fence on the way back. The noise was comforting, reassuring.

Sometimes, Nicola and I would lie on our backs in the long grass beside a pond in the top garden. It must have been summertime by now, it was warm. We seemed to have been incarcerated forever in that prison. I never remember my grandparents visiting us, no one came. Looking up at the blue sky, filled with clouds, we would watch the birds so free; soaring, singing, unrestrained. .

My earliest culinary memory is refusing to eat tapioca pudding one day at lunchtime. It was gloopy, sticky and lumpy and just would not go down my throat. It smelled – perhaps it had been burned. So I was sent to my dormitory again, until my plate was clean. Very Victorian. I still remember the total isolation, the sense of unfairness, being trapped in a room, excluded.

Chapter 10

Release

We were rescued from this awful place by a pretty blonde woman called Jocelyn. She introduced herself, saying, "Very soon we shall be sailing back to Colombo. I am coming with you. We are all going back to see your father." This was music to our ears; we both were so excited. She scooped Nicola and me up, taking us to Chipstead, where my father's mother, Granny Burns, now lived. We were ecstatic, running around in Granny's beautiful garden, savouring complete freedom, before we boarded another Bibby Line boat. This time our long four-week journey would have a happy ending.

Jocelyn Hammond had been born in 1921 in Colombo. She and her younger sister, Gill, were brought up in a typical Dutch bungalow, designed with heavy shutters, surrounded by a veranda on two sides. It stood under palm trees in a large garden, near the sea at the end of one of the narrow lanes leading downhill off the Galle Road, close to St Andrew's church. This was one of the first areas which had been settled by the Dutch. It must have been idyllic, living so close to the sea and yet near the Galle Face Hotel and some of the shops. Her father, nicknamed Hammy, had an engineering business servicing heavy machinery used to manufacture tea.

Her mother Muriel was a leading light in the amateur dramatics scene, friendly with Lionel Wendt whose name was given to the first theatre in Colombo.

Jocelyn and Gill had been taught at home with a governess until they also had been bundled off to boarding school in Suffolk. At the time, Jocelyn was barely ten. "It was horrible," she used to say. "Gilly and I were always cold at school, the wind just blew and blew and blew. Granny was very strict with us during the holidays. She lived in Walberswick. I hated being in England. We both were very homesick. But we had each other." Certainly she was empathetic to our plight and tried to make life happy for us both.

She had met my father at a party, and obviously fancied this darkly handsome man. When she heard my mother had died, she wrote to him with commiserations and she and Gary struck up a friendship through correspondence. This went on for some time. Her first marriage, to an army officer, which had taken her to Delhi and Karachi, had come unstuck. Now she was working near Godalming, in Surrey, where her cousins were living. When she wrote to say she was planning to sail back to Colombo to visit her parents, he replied, "Would you consider bringing my daughters out with you?" Many years later she confessed: "Gary never even paid for my ticket."

Jocelyn must have brave, perhaps already in love, longing to return to Colombo, to agree to escort Nicola and me, two children she had never met. Also, she had had no experience in dealing with youngsters. This was to change very quickly.

This boat trip was much more fun, already my third

and I was just five years old. Jocelyn was artistic. When she realised there was to be a fancy dress competition for all the children, she dressed me up as a chocolate box. Goodness knows where she found the blue crinkly cellophane paper. She spent hours carefully covering cardboard, bending it to make a box. She made a huge bow out of the same translucent paper and, somehow, put me inside. It was dark and hot but I was determined to do my best. I was enjoying all the attention. At the parade, pirates, fairies and other imaginatively dressed children walked around the deck, but I won first prize. Jocelyn was thrilled for me, it was extremely special. It was the first prize I remember winning.

For us, arriving back to the heat and brightness of this glorious tropical island, seeing our father again after an absence of nearly a year, made me realise this place was heaven, even at my young age. No more cold, dark evenings, uncomfortable nights full of nightmares, food being forced down my throat, or loneliness with Nicola and I clinging to each other in desperation. It was an end to separation from our beloved father. He very quickly married Jocelyn and the four of us went to live in a house called Minster, in Jawatta Road, just south of the smart area of Cinnamon Gardens, close to the racecourse. Before the start of the housing boom, when it had been decided to build a harbour in order to make Colombo the new capital, this area of gently rolling countryside had been covered with cinnamon trees.

Chapter 11

Life at Minster

Birdsong woke me every morning along with the swish, swish, swish of the garden coolie's ekel broom, and the fisherman's musical call – "malu, malu, malu" – as he trundled down the avenue, laden with fish box and weighing scales. The chicken man carried two baskets of chickens, tied to both ends of a pole slung across his shoulders. He advertised his wares, calling loudly above the cries of his hens, as did the milkman and the scrap merchant.

Thimbrigasaya, at the end of Jawatta Road, was where the racing stables had been built. Every day we heard the clip-clop, clip-clop, as several strings of elegantly groomed horses passed by, being led to the racecourse for their morning practice. Just before breakfast we heard them returning. We would run to the gate to watch these beautiful creatures, now hot after their exertions, their backs covered with light coats, returning to their stables. We had our favourites and would call and wave as the grooms led them past. Horse racing was extremely popular and fashionable, even in the heat.

This big, square house, Minster, had a large frangipani or temple tree in the garden close to the high, ivy-clad wall on Jawatta Road. These white fragrant blooms with pale yellow at their centres decorated the grass like stars when they dropped from the spreading tree. Some early mornings we watched as poles with a curved knife at the end were lifted from the roadside to cut the blooms from large branches leaning over the road. These invisible pluckers took these gloriously scented flowers as offerings to the temple. More likely, they were woven into garlands and sold.

Our morning walks had to be finished before the heat became too much. Afterwards, ayah would wash our hair, then instruct us to sit under the shade of the glossy-leaved mango tree which shaded the upstairs veranda. She merely combed out our hair, placed a towel around our shoulders and made us sit still for five minutes. It was very hot. She would wash, iron and tidy our clothes, help us to put on our cotton sundresses, do up our white leather sandals, get ready for bed, and tidy our rooms.

Chapter 12

Party Time

Nicola and I sometimes went to afternoon parties. Dressed up in our best printed cotton frocks, both made to match, bows in our neatly brushed hair, the rickshaw man would be called. Waiting in the driveway, he greeted us with a salaam, placing his hands together, smiling. He was always used by our family. He held his rickshaw steady, the tips of the arm handles on the ground as Nicola, ayah and I climbed up the high step to sit close together on the slippery, hard seat. We braced ourselves as this strong, lean-legged, barefoot man with his white sarong tucked up between his legs slowly lifted the handles, allowing us to lean back in the seat. Steadying himself, holding the handles to balance his heavy load, he walked out of the gate, turning left into Jawatta Road.

Checking for traffic and keeping close to the edge of the road, he broke into a gentle run, pulling us along behind him. It was safer then, in 1950. There were not many cars on the streets and it was a pleasant way to travel with warm air blowing through our hair, whiffs of frangipani catching our nostrils. It was exhilarating, the accepted way of transport. At the junction with Bullers Road he turned right, up a gently sloping incline past Spittals Home, then Coniston Place, where our friends lived, the Ceylon Broadcasting Station, Maitland Place and finally, left into Gregory's Avenue. Ayah gave directions to the house. At our destination, gently putting his handles onto the ground which made the rickshaw tilt forward, the puller turned around to help us climb down. Now he would wait outside on the grass verge with the other rickshaw owners, until we were ready to go home.

We had arrived at a large mansion in one of the smartest parts of Colombo. This was the rental home of Mr Exeter, the head of the American bank. His son, Buffy, was Nicola's age and today was his birthday party. The grand entrance opened onto extensive green lawns completely surrounding the house. Mature trees surrounded the walls, protecting its privacy. Ferns, anthuriums, mother-in-law's tongues (*sansevieria*) stood in large pots decorating the outside veranda which ran the length of the front of the house. Steps from the garden led up onto this veranda where cane chairs were arranged in a semi-circle. Some mothers in pretty full-skirted afternoon sundresses were sitting drinking tea; the men, in cream trousers, short white shirts and ties, already with drinks in hand, were exchanging business news, standing together under the fan.

The afternoon was humid; sloping sun rays filtered through the trees, hitting the backs of the seats, the men's trousers. A uniformed waiter stood quietly by a side table, silver tray in hand, waiting to fill the glasses, refill tea cups and hand round cakes. A buzz of excitement filled the air.

Ayah walked with us over the neatly clipped grass to where a small crowd of boys and girls had gathered around Buffy. His presents lay scattered on the ground, discarded brightly coloured wrapping paper and ribbons beside his feet. He wore a red spotted bow tie with his white pressed shirt. Animated, perspiring, arms waving around him, he was regaling his friends with a story, the small crowd attentive. Once we had safely joined the group we gave Buffy his present. "Yeah, thanks," he said. His American accent was strong, and he quickly tore off the paper, carrying on with his story.

Ayah told us she was going to the back of the house until she was needed to take us home. I could hear the clink of cups from the veranda, laughter from the men. It was comforting to be there, an accepted part of the group, feeling safe, full of anticipation. The heady scent of evening jasmine growing over the side of the garden wall was already filling the air. Nicola kept close beside me, chewing her fingers. Already I had sensed I needed to keep an eye on her, watching in case she had a fit, and to make sure she didn't wander off. She was now a whole head taller than me.

It was soon time for the Gully Gully Man. No party was complete without this local magician. He stood nearby, quiet, self-contained, a country man in shirt and dhoti, holding a small sack and basket. Mr Exeter called him over to join our group. Putting his lidded basket on the ground in front of him, pulling a pipe from his bag as he sat cross-legged on the grass, the Gully Gully Man began to play entrancing music, his body moving with the rhythm, his eyes closed. With a slight nod, he motioned to us to gather close to him. The chatter from the veranda ceased, cups were put down, heads turned to watch. We all stood silently, expectantly, holding our breath, knowing what was going to happen. Even the birds had stopped their singing – there was total hush. The notes stretched out, exotic, plaintive, floating in the air. Suddenly, the basket lid began to move, at first cautiously, then more firmly, until it came off, pushed by the cobra's head, its forked tongue darting in and out, its large black eye visible on the back of its head. We all gasped. The music carried on enticingly, the man seemingly in a trance. The cobra extended its long, sensual neck and looked around, moving high out of its basket, gracefully curving its long, shiny body, moving in time with the rhythmic notes of the flute, swaying from side to side. We gazed, fascinated. Apart from the flute, there was complete silence; no one moved.

Putting down his instrument, the Gully Gully Man slowly picked up the cobra out of the basket. Holding his long snake firmly with both hands, one on the tail and one behind its head, he moved towards us. Everyone in the group instinctively moved backwards. I was entranced. He stopped in front of me. Smiling, he gently placed the snake behind my neck. Standing still, in shock, I hardly dared breathe. He made another turn of the snake's body until it was lying completely around my neck. The other children were staring. The cobra felt heavy, cool, smooth. It lay still, wrapped around my neck, imprisoned by his master's strong arms. I wasn't sure where the forked tongue was. I didn't want to know. We both stood immobile, the other children now gasping and laughing. Someone took a photograph. I was glad when he untwisted his pet and put it back into the basket with the lid firmly on.

His sack was lying on the ground. Squatting down on his heels beside it, he bent, pressing the sack firmly so we could see there was nothing inside. Again he picked up his flute and started playing evocatively. What was going to happen? Was the sack moving? No, there was nothing inside. We moved forward to get a closer look. The sack seemed to be rising up, gently, slowly, getting taller and fuller, higher and higher, as he carried on playing. We were all mystified. Still the sack grew, still he played. Suddenly, he stopped. With both hands he lifted the sack up and off with a flourish. There was a small tree. Green leaves moving in the slight breeze. We stared, unbelieving. Later, I was told it was an avocado tree. It certainly hadn't been there before he started. In amazement we all laughed and clapped, turning to each other, exclaiming. Smiling, he put his sack and cobra basket into his bag, melting away into the crowd.

On the grass at the side of this grand garden were our favourite tea rollers. We always begged our parents to have them at our parties. These metal rollers were used in tea factories to push the chests, when heavily filled with fragrant tea, to the lorries. Here they had been set up, high at one end, sloping downwards, curved around like a small railway. Steps allowed us to climb up to the high end where, one by one, we clambered into an empty wooden chest. The box felt hard. I sat in the bottom, holding tightly onto the sides, breathing in that evocative, lingering tea smell. One of the helpers pushed me off. Down I went, faster and faster, the rollers clacking and spinning, making high, rumbling, squeaking sounds; then around the corner, along the straight until I stopped with a thump at the bottom. It was such fun. Climbing out onto the grass I ran back to the end of the queue to have another turn.

Chapter 13

Vogan Estate

We were, by now, used to Nicola's frequent fits, all of us extremely protective towards her. To me she was my big sister, always there with me, doing what I asked her with an unquestioning obedience. I am sure I must have been unkind to her, taking advantage, bossing her around. Nicola found it hard to learn so she had a special teacher, Nora Cade, whose house she went to in the mornings.

When our rent was due for renewal on Minster, the large house we had been living in on Jawatta Road, my father decided that for a few months we would live as paying guests on a low country tea and rubber estate called Vogan. Perhaps our doctor, Dr Van Langenberg, had advised cooler air and plenty of space for running around as being beneficial for Nicola. Perhaps Lee Hedges were agents for this estate as he and Farqui, the manager, were friends. I don't know. From there he commuted daily to his office in Colombo. It was a long, twisty journey for him.

Vogan was another paradise. A smooth lawn, dotted with flowering bushes, sloped away from the manager's bungalow with a thick hibiscus hedge separating the garden from the intense greenness of the surrounding tea fields. Unevenly topped blue-green hills formed a backdrop to all this lushness. The late afternoons were cool, peaceful. We sat on the veranda, drinking tea, rich and fresh from the factory, looking out towards the distant skyline. After a day in the tea fields, Farqui taught me simple card games while I sat on a leather pouffe at his side. He wore long thick white socks up to his knobbly suntanned knees, khaki shorts and an open-necked shirt. He always had a pipe clenched between his teeth. Perhaps he reminded me of my grandfather, puffing away, allowing us all to breathe in his tobacco smoke. I loved him, despite his gruffness. He was very patient and gave Nicola and me time.

Nicola loved Farqui's Peter and Paul game. He stuck a small piece of paper on both his index fingers, chanting, "Two little dicky birds sitting on a wall, one named Peter, one named Paul. Fly away, Peter…" Farqui quickly changed fingers so there was no 'bird' when his finger returned. The same happened with Paul. "Come back, Peter," he said and miraculously, the bird reappeared. Nicola laughed and laughed, asking Farqui to repeat his game over and over.

Ayah took us on early morning walks, down the bumpy gravel drive, past red and yellow flowering hibiscus bushes which edged the back lawn, through the gate, onto the estate road. The air was cool and fresh, unlike the heavy humidity we had become used to in Colombo. This part of the country was renowned for enormous rock boulders, strewn down the hillsides as though a giant had scattered them during a temper. We gave some of them names.

The altitude was perfect for growing rubber. Trees had

been planted in rows, like soldiers marching down the hill, line after line. Rough grass and stones lay between the trees, the biggest boulders having been removed before planting. Arduous work. The narrow trunks curved gracefully, all bending the same way, their upper branches providing a light green, cooling canopy over the trunks.

The rubber tappers were already at work. We stopped to watch. Ayah greeted one close to us, carrying on a spirited conversation in Sinhala. We heard her say, "Missy Nicola, Missy Judy," so perhaps she was telling them who we were. The tapper bent down to pull the dried latex off the old cut, then using a sharp knife, he cut a downwards spiral in the trunk below the line made by all the previous incisions, throwing small, unwanted pieces of bark and stringy latex onto the ground. At the base of the cut, half a coconut shell had been attached to the tree to catch the sticky, oozing white sap. The tapper removed the cup, emptying the latex into his large container, and moved to the next tree. Week after week, month after month, year after year, this process was repeated, the old cut area of bark large and dark against the smooth, tapering trunk.

A young boy approached us with something in his hands. "It's a baby bird," I squeaked in excitement. "Is it alive? Please, can we keep it?" Ayah exchanged a few words. "He thinks it's fallen out of the nest. It's a mynah bird." I could hardly contain myself as he placed the tiny, shivering creature into my hands. It was so soft, its wings smooth, quite defenceless. Its beak was bright yellow. I had never held a wild bird in my hands before. "Why don't you put it into your hat and we can carry it back," said ayah. We found an old shoe box which Nicola and I lined with cotton wool. Gently, we placed the tiny creature in its new home. We spent the whole day watching the terrified bird hunched in the corner of its box. We tried to give it liquid through a medicine dropper which ayah had found in a drawer. It cheeped weakly, probably preferring a few juicy worms. I longed for it to grow so I could teach it to talk. The following morning we found it lying feet upward, quite still and cold. We buried it under a bush in the garden.

Chapter 14

Another tragedy

Nicola and I slept side by side in twin beds. One morning I awoke with a start. Something had alerted me. It was very early, that time when darkness turns grey before becoming light. Thin white cotton curtains separating the bedroom from the front veranda were blowing gently in the breeze, softening the concrete floor and black window frames. I sat up, looking over at Nicola's bed. I looked again, unable to believe what I could see. She appeared to be covered in spittle from head to toe and was lying motionless. "Nicola?" I called. "Nico, Nico?" I shouted, feeling alarmed. No response.

Jumping onto the cool floor I ran through the curtains onto the veranda and into our parents' room next door, shaking them awake. "Quick, quick. It's Nicola – she's had a fit." We were used to these, but nothing had been like this before. I was scared. My father took control. "Climb into my bed and snuggle down," he said, but I couldn't relax. My heart was beating too fast. I heard them talking loudly in the next room – their concern, the phone calls, the servant's swish of feet and sarong as the tea tray was put on the veranda table, the rattle of cups. Now Farqui's voice, strong, reassuring, calming them.

My ayah, comforting in her presence, came in with my

clothes. "Come, get dressed, Missy Judy. Daddy has called the ambulance and the doctor is coming." She helped with the buttons on my dress, giving me a reassuring hug. "What about Nicola?" I asked. There was no answer to give.

Later that day ayah and I stood side by side. She held my hand. I watched as Nicola, strapped onto a stretcher, was gently lifted into the ambulance. She appeared to be sleeping. My parents hugged me and climbed in after her. Nothing was said. The doors were closed. The ambulance moved slowly, rocking over the bumps, down the drive, stirring the dust. They were off to Colombo.

Once more we all boarded ship to sail to distant, cold England. This time Nicola was in the sick bay. Every day I went to talk to her, to try to make sense of what was happening around me. My head came up to the level of the white-painted metal bars around her bed, which were fixed to stop her climbing out. They had been wrapped with thin gauze bandages to stop Nicola biting the paint. I looked at her through this grille. She writhed in the bed, muttering, not appearing to know who I was. Her hands stretched out, touching the bell, which had to be disconnected. She clawed the bars like a wild animal in a cage. My heart was broken – my big sister had gone to another world. I couldn't touch her, hold her, comfort her. The nurse fussed around. Nobody explained to me what was happening.

We arrived back in England again where Nicola was taken to London, to the National Hospital for Nervous Diseases. I went to stay with Granny Burns, who now was living in Reigate, not too far from London. After a few days the doctors said they could do nothing for her. They suggested the heat in Ceylon would be too much for her, that perhaps she would be better off staying in a temperate climate. My father must have gone through hell trying to make the right choice for his family. His work was in Colombo, 6,000 miles away. Finally, however, a decision was made, although at the time I was too young to truly understand the consequences of their actions.

My big sister was going to be left 'in care' at the tender age of seven and a half. A small, friendly home, providing care for children like Nicola, was found in Haywards Heath, in Sussex. It was run by a Mrs Farrer Brown who had other youngsters in her care. She was a warm and loving woman.

Looking back now, nearly sixty years ago, when neurosurgery was in its infancy and medical care in Ceylon for Nicola's problems was limited, my father simply had no choice. Our hearts were broken, as this time, only three of us boarded the ship to sail back to the tropics. Nicola never returned to Ceylon.

Chapter 15

Jawatta Avenue

Back in Colombo, despite missing my sister, I felt very at home with the smells, sounds, brilliant sun and warmth. Every day my father was driven to his office in the Galle Road, and my stepmother ran the house with a cook, house boy and garden coolie. The house we were renting this time stood at the end of the right-hand side of Jawatta Avenue, a short cul-de-sac close to where we were living before in Minster. It had two storeys, although it was referred to as a bungalow, always dark and gloomy and protected by tall trees. Mosquitoes abounded under these trees, in the creepers which surrounded and climbed up the trunks. Thick-bladed short grass grew on two sides of this Dutch-style house.

Now I had a new ayah. A burgher, a mixture of Ceylonese and Portuguese or Dutch blood, Noeline had light-coloured skin. She wore cotton dresses, had a crucifix around her neck and, even at age five, I realised that she was different to the sari-clad ayah I had loved before we took Nicola to England. She spoke English well, could read me stories, was firm with me and also a companion. It was strange without Nicola's presence. We were all trying to get used to being without her.

Noeline often sang to me; she had a beautiful voice.

She would sit me on her lap. Many of these songs seemed to be sad, all about love. My favourite, the one which I still remember best, must have been a hit in the early fifties: "Give me five minutes more, only five minutes more; let me stay, let me stay, in your arms." I often pondered over the words, singing the rhyme to myself, wondering why she would want to stay so long in someone's arms. I knew nothing about boys breaking girls' hearts, but certainly I was a sad child, missing my sister. But I loved Noeline. We did everything together; she was there for me, and I enjoyed sitting on her lap, feeling comfortable.

From memory, my stepmother seemed to play a very small part in this period of my life. She had her own problems to deal with. Much later I learned that she was trying very hard to conceive a baby but it never happened for her. Every month she took to her bed with terrible pains. Nowadays it is called endometriosis and help is available. Poor Jocelyn, how she must have suffered. My father was having his own health problems as well, his asthma attacks becoming more frequent. He had been prescribed a new wonder drug called cortisone, but no one knew then how severe the side effects would be. Jocelyn's father, whom we called Hammy, was staying with us, winding up his business in Colombo before retiring back to the UK. He slept downstairs where he had his own bathroom and sitting room.

One night my father was rushed to hospital with a suspected heart attack, probably brought on by all the stress he had been under and, possibly, this new drug. I remember so clearly my panic in the darkness; it was late and there was silence in the house. "Don't worry," said Uncle Hammy, "he will be home soon." He came upstairs to keep me company. I was inconsolable, scared again, certain that now my father would die and I would have to go back on that ship again, thousands of miles away, pulled apart from everything that was safe for me.

Sometime later my father returned home and life returned to some sort of normalcy, but from then on I was very protective towards him. I didn't want him to die like my mother. He wheezed when he breathed, always after exercise, often when he was tired. Sometimes it was very loud. He would sit with his shoulders hunched up, struggling for breath. He used his squeegee many times a day, when he was short of breath. It lived in a grey cylindrical tin, with a screw-on cap. He took it everywhere with him. He would lean his elbows on a chest, or on the banister, or some other suitable place, unscrew his tin, take out the contraption which had a black rubber bulb on the bottom, and put his lips around the brown glass mouthpiece. Then, breathing out first, he would rapidly squeeze the bulb three times, while he breathed in deeply. A fine spray was released into his lungs. This medication helped to relax his chest, enabling him to breathe more easily. He always coughed when he finished. Squish, squish, squish, morning, noon and night, day in, day out, my father had to use it. We knew how well he was by the amount of times he used his squeegee.

I decided I was going to make some healing herbs for him. I was determined to make him better. Walking around the garden, I picked several leaves and flowers, drying them in the sun. Crumbling them up, I stored them in a pot which I kept in my room.

My father came home for lunch then retired to his bedroom for a siesta.

I knocked on the door. "Come in," he said. I wasn't allowed in without knocking. There he was, shoes and socks off, belt loosened, lying propped up, as always, breathing heavily with a big effort. "Daddy," I said, walking towards the bed. "I have something to make you better." He smiled at me. "I am going to sprinkle some medicine over you to help you to breathe more easily." I had my special pot with me. Opening it, I gently scattered some of the fragrant dried concoction over him. "Now you will get better!"

"Thank you very much, darling. Now I know I shall have a very good snooze before I go back to the office. Off you go. I shall see you at tea time." He closed his eyes, probably hating the smell. The dried flowers and leaves may have made him worse; I shall never know. I crept out. My darling pa, so gentle, so loving, always thinking of others, struggling all his life for breath, never complaining. Little did I realise that all the suffering I had experienced was the start of a lifelong journey for me.

Chapter 16

Bicycle Trips

I had learned to ride a bicycle with my grandparents, Grandpa holding the back of my seat, standing on top of a sloped road running down from the canal bridge at Ash Vale. Gently he had let me go. Suddenly, I had been able to keep my balance. The sensation of controlled movement was wonderful. My parents had bought me one on return to Colombo. Each morning, Noeline would be on her bike, keeping close behind me and I would bicycle down the Bullers Road. Here spreading rain trees formed a high arch over the road, cathedral like, blocking out strong sunlight. At the roundabout, we turned right into Reid Avenue, where we had to be careful as the traffic was heavier, then left into Thurstan Road, past the university playing fields, then left again, bicycling down Queens Road. We were nearly there.

"Careful, Judy. Not too fast," called Noeline, as I had speeded up, sensing the end of the journey. Traffic noise receded. Here it was peaceful, this residential street lined by garden walls of large houses. Rain-water ditches ran along both sides. Sparse grass grew at the margins where the leaves and rubbish had already been swept up into tidy piles.

Our destination was at the end of Queens Avenue, a

tiny lane, scarcely wide enough for a car. The downstairs of a substantial house with French windows opening onto a smooth, manicured lawn had been given over to our nursery school. Tall trees, brightly flowering shrubs, red ixora, orange hibiscus, yellow allamanda, growing close to the high creeper-clad walls, held a mass of sunbirds, darting, feasting on the nectar.

Noeline returned at twelve o'clock to escort me home for lunch. We passed moving strings of bicycles, each one piled high with tiffin boxes on the back pillions. These were aluminium bowls, their lids held on with a white cloth, tied on the top. At the large crossroads the cyclists went in every direction, taking curry lunches to office workers.

After my sleep, freshly dressed in one of my afternoon sundresses and open-toed sandals, Noeline took me for a walk down Jawatta Road, sometimes to a small graveyard, where wide paths under the trees and a grassy hillock provided space for me to run around. Tall flame of the forest trees reached to the sky. I bent down to collect red seeds from the long, curved pods which had fallen onto the ground under these statuesque trees. I marvelled at their size and colour. In downtown Pettah, the suq area beyond the smart Fort shopping district of Colombo, was an elderly man who carved tiny ivory elephants. He put many of these into a red seed, completing his work with a minute ivory stopper. I studied these seeds, wondering how he managed something so fiddly.

Crows were always lined up in the overhead branches with their shiny black beaks, cawing loudly, repetitively, noisily, grating, rasping, disturbing the peace. Always on the lookout for food, eyeing us suspiciously, they flew to adjacent trees with a great flap of wings, claws tucked under their streamlined bodies, when we came close by. Still cawing, they resumed their vigil, their incessant calling: the sound of my childhood.

Sometimes we saw a bier being carried along the road, a dead person on top, covered by a white sheet. The mourners walked behind, chanting, all dressed in white. I was fascinated, and stared at these simple rites. It looked so informal. For an important funeral, strips of fresh coconut leaves would be suspended from coir rope, hung along the route. White sheets would be hung outside the houses past which the procession came. Jocelyn complained to the dhobi, our washerman: "What are these small holes in my sheets?" She pointed to tiny holes in each corner. "Lady…" He would look away, shifting from foot to foot, unwilling to own up, hoping she may understand. Perhaps he rented these sheets to mourners, to eke out his living.

All over Colombo we saw washing hanging to dry, stiff and hard under the burning sun, draped on grass, over bushes and small trees, even on coir lines.

On other days we walked down Jawatta Road, turning right into an area where large detached houses surrounded by sizeable gardens, protected with tall, spreading shade trees, were surrounded by a grassy square. The three Hooper boys lived in one of these houses. Longingly I looked through their gate when I saw them shouting and playing in their garden, missing my sister, wishing to be part of a big family. Sometimes I was invited in by them.

It was peaceful in the afternoon sun, sitting on the

grass, even though it was scratchy, very prickly and dry, full of ants. I searched for patches of small dark-green leaves of the sensitive plant, feeling it gently, watching the leaves shrivel up under my touch, as I looked out to see whether other children were coming to play, allowing our ayahs to sit together, to gossip.

On the corner of the square I often saw two women sitting together, one parting the other's hair, using fingers to remove, crack and kill head lice and remove the nits. This activity could be seen anywhere: on the edge of the pavement, beside a house; whenever women had a few spare moments together. Singhalese women all had long, dark hair, well lubricated with coconut oil, making the job easier. Noeline searched for nits in my hair frequently, using a fine comb, pulling it hard, taking out the black eggs, after which she applied foul-smelling lotion. Then I was told to sleep with a towel on my pillow, waiting until morning for a hair wash.

Chapter 17

Colombo Swimming Club

Around about this time I became a member of the Colombo Swimming Club, in Galle Road, just opposite Temple Trees, the prime minister's residence. This place became my second home. Sometimes the driver would drop me by the main entrance. Picking up my towel roll from the car seat, I would climb the steps and walk over the polished wooden floor of the entrance hall, where formally arranged flowers stood at the base of the grand staircase. I loved to look at this multitude of colour – tall, pointed gladioli, red anthuriums, sweet-smelling tuber roses grown in the cool of the hills. A doorkeeper, dressed in white jacket and sarong complete with a tortoiseshell hair ring, would smile at me in recognition, saying, "Good morning, missy." I could smell beeswax polish on the shiny wooden floor. Through the French doors, beyond the lounge, a breeze laden with sea air came straight off the Indian Ocean, which stretched as far as the eye could see. Beyond the terrace – past the smooth, clipped grass replete with deck chairs, umbrellas and tables – was the pool.

It never failed to excite me. Sparkling, blue, enticing water where the springboard stood at the deep end, the three- and five-metre boards close by. A three-tiered water fountain splashed ceaselessly between the pool and sea wall. Its constant rushing, tumbling sound was almost deafening, as cooled water spray wet the surrounding tiles, making them brown and slippery. Get too close and you could smell the powerful chlorine smell spewing out from the water. Behind the high wall, smut-stained brown trains frequently rumbled past, en route from Fort station down towards Galle in the south. Passengers clung onto the sides of the open doors, straining to see over the wall. Our parents always warned us not to go too close to the wall: "Someone might pull you over with their umbrella handle." Did this happen once?

I walked, full of anticipation, through the lounge and down the steps to the darkness of the ladies' changing room. Brown coir matting, rough underfoot, stretched the length of the room. White curtained cubicles stood on each side. The mangle stood in a corner beside the mirrors, waiting for us to squeeze the water from our wet costumes. The handle was always stiff. There was a damp, dank smell in there. A diminutive Singhalese woman, dressed in white, smiled at me "Good morning, missy" as I asked her to help me undo the top buttons of my sundress. I never knew or asked her name. With her black hair tied into a bun, gold earrings and betel-stained teeth, she was known as ayah. She was always there, comforting in her presence, keeping a maternal eye on us young girls.

Shrugging off my cotton dress and slipping on my costume, I went to the outside shower, the water always cold against my skin, even in that humid climate. The concrete tiles were burning hot, knobbly under my feet as I walked quickly to the Olympic-sized pool.

Harry Nightingale, once an Australian Olympic swimmer, taught all of us to swim. Harry was an institution. Ageless, he was as brown as a berry, gentle in manner, his worn straw hat always visible as he walked across the widths, quietly talking to his pupil.

Today was my lesson. "Come on, Judy Anne," he would say. He never knew my correct name. "Touch your thumb to the side of your hip, like this. You can do it." Lying on the pool's hot edge, face turned sideways, pressed into the gritty surface of the tile, swinging my arm on the pool side around and around, he would gently push my thumb onto my hip, correcting my movements, before telling me to turn around to practise on the other side. Then I would slither into the water and hold the edge with my fingers, feeling the tile ridges on the soles of my feet. "Lie on your tummy now, Judy Anne. Slowly, give me your arms." I lay in the strongly chlorinated water, always confident with this caring man. Harry faced me, walking backwards, catching each fingertip as I struggled to kick my legs, to keep my body straight, turn my head, blow out bubbles, keep my eyes open under water and swing my arms, all in the correct sequence. He was a marvellous teacher, so patient, appearing to have all the time in the world.

We loved our lessons with Harry and many of his pupils went on to become well-known swimmers. When he retired his battered hat was placed in a glass-fronted box on the wall beside all the notices.

At home my father was strict with me. First he taught me always to rinse my costume and cap properly; the chlorine was so strong it quickly ate into both rubber and material. Then I had to hang up my towel and costume on the line, using clothes pegs. Next he put my *Girl* comic on the bottom of the bathroom basin, filling it with water: "Put your face in, keep your eyes open, see what you can read." I didn't dare to disobey him but I dreaded this and hated doing it. The pictures were blurry; the water stung my eyes, got up my nose. It was his way of teaching me to keep my eyes open under water. Perhaps he remembered the wonderful swimmer my mother had been and wanted me to emulate her.

Chapter 18

My Stepmother

Life was not always comfortable. I was an only child and very angry. I was sad, grieving. I had lost my mother, my sister, and was unable to voice my innermost feelings. Now my stepmother was coming between my father and me. I sensed him distancing himself, going to his office every day, leaving me with a person I did not want around. He and I were so alike. I am sure I played on this, being moody and difficult. It must have been hard for her. Despite my nature, she tried to be a good mother to me. Pretty, blonde, always dressed in softly patterned sundresses, she took me to Hirdaramanis, in Chatham Street. Taking off my dress in a hot enclosed room, the plump tailor lifted a half-formed garment over my head. He always smelled of sweat. I held my breath. "Please turn, missy," he said, through a mouth full of pins. Obediently, I stood still, gently turning around, sweat trickling down my back, while he put pins into the cloth, sometimes pricking. The finished results were light and comfortable; I had morning and afternoon dresses.

Afterwards we went to the Sundae Tea Rooms. This was my biggest treat. Walking through swing doors, we could see small circular tables under the fans. Behind a high counter, on the left, stood jars of flavouring, shelves of glasses, with high stools in front. Well-thumbed narrow cream menus stood on each table, pictures displaying all their delicacies. Ice cream soda was my favourite. A tall iced glass, full to the brim with vanilla ice cream, two straws sticking out of the top, standing on a plate complete with paper doily, was placed in front of me. I watched bubbles rising around the scoops of ice cream, felt the cold glass. "Thank you, Mummy." I smiled at her, before firmly sticking the straw through the thick ice cream until it hit the bottom of the glass. Then I took my first long, cool, sweet suck. This was heaven. Ice cream lined my mouth, cooling and soothing me. I forgot the smelly tailor and his hot room. My mother had a cup of tea. I sucked and sucked, trying to savour every last cold drop. Tilting my nearly empty glass, I made a big slurp to suck up the last whiteness. "Judy Jane, be quiet please. That is very rude!" she said. "Sorry, Mummy. This is so lovely," I replied. My second name was always used by my parents when they were displeased with me. I hated my name. Once I asked my father why he had chosen them: "Your mother and I pulled them out of a hat!" I used to believe him, but as I grew older I realised it was just my father's manner.

My mother's days revolved around organising the servants. After breakfast she sat in the cool, dark pantry with the cook, discussing the menu. I looked in to see what they were doing. They were discussing what was needed from the market. Cookie was standing, my mother sitting, reading Cookie's accounts book, which she checked each week. There were always problems; the figures somehow didn't balance. She sighed heavily; she was nervous, imperious, impatient. Cookie's perks were what extra he could make out of the cash she gave him. "Judy Jane, leave us alone. Go upstairs please."

Each morning, after her stint with the cook, my mother would sit by the phone, making her orders from the Elephant House cold stores. I can see her now, beside the black banisters, sitting on a wooden foam-covered stool next to the small phone table. Light streamed in from the open veranda behind her, lighting up her wavy blonde hair and pretty sundress. It was cool in this upstairs hallway. Her book, containing all the numbers and her shopping list, sat on her lap. Our phone was heavy, made from black bakelite. Leaning against the wall, handkerchief smelling of lavender water in one hand, phone in the other, she dialled, asked for the department she needed, giving her name, phone number, address, followed by her order, slowly, clearly. It took a long time; she had to repeat herself many times, spelling words over again, speaking louder and louder, becoming more frustrated by the poor language skills of whoever was taking her order. "S-h-a-t-t-o-c-k... No, S-h-a... Yes! Mrs. E.C.E...Yes..." She wiped her forehead, sighed, crossed and uncrossed her legs.

In my bedroom, close by, I listened, fascinated. Sixty years later, I can hear her now and am sure I learned to spell many words listening to our daily orders. I still remember our number, 8448, later changed to 816448.

Chapter 19

Shopping

"Judy Jane, I am going to Colpetty market today. Would you like to come?" I loved this market, with its brightly coloured vegetable and fruit stands. Our tame fruit man spoiled me with sweet, small yellow bananas, sometimes even a mangosteen. He knew these were my favourite. Strong, overpowering smells wafted from the fish stalls, and close by lines of bright red meat hung from hooks, covered by flies, blood dripping to the earth. Colpetty was on the way to the pool; I hoped I would be taken there afterwards for a swim.

Our green Morris Minor, EY1139, was my father's pride and joy. He loved to tinker over the engine at weekends. Now he had risen to a position in his office where he was entitled to a driver. So my mother and I, hotly squashed in the back seat, were driven off to the market. If I was lucky we carried on to the swimming club, where I ran to change and she sat under the shade, sipping her tea.

Sometimes we went to the Fort for shopping, past my father's office, down the Galle Road, past the green and the parliament building. Cargills, Apothecaries and Whiteaways were the three large all-purpose stores standing on York Street. As the driver negotiated an angled parking spot, beggars sidled up to the windows, hands outstretched, often a small baby hugged to their hips. They whined, putting on a desperate face for our white skins. My mother always ignored them. I felt uncomfortable, uneasy.

"Please wait here; we shall be half an hour."

"Yes, lady," our driver, Peter, a Christian, replied obediently, as he opened the doors for us. I always felt sorry for him, waiting for us in the sun. My heart sank as I climbed out, following my mother. An elderly, country Singhalese woman, hair coiled into a bun, gold ring in her nose, standing in the shady arcade, accosted us, holding a delicately embroidered lace tablecloth in her arms. She stretched it out, the lace catching the light. "Lady, please buy. I am very poor. Lady, look, look." I looked: they were pretty cloths. She also had skeins of lace lying across her shoulders. This woman was poor, her face lined, her teeth stained red with betel juice, a pleading look in her eyes. My mother walked past her, brushing her off, as I trailed behind, feeling sad for the woman, as we entered into the red-brick Cargills building.

Inside endless glass counters displaying their wares filled the space. My mother walked around; looking, looking. I dutifully walked after her, never quite knowing what she wanted to buy. Behind each counter was a salesgirl dressed in her brightly coloured short choli (blouse) and sari. I leaned against the counter while she spoke with these pretty assistants. It was boring and hot. "Judy, stand up. Don't scratch." Today, she was searching for elastic. By now we had climbed the stairs to the second floor. It was darker up there. Finding what she wanted, mother handed the roll to the salesgirl, who measured and cut the elastic. She laboriously wrote a receipt, taking a twenty-rupee note from my mother. Putting one copy of the receipt and the note into a metal cylinder, fastening the lid, she placed the cylinder into a pipe, then closed the top. With a woosh and clank, it vanished. The rolled-up length of elastic was placed on a second copy of the receipt, on the side of the counter. The paper flapped from the breeze of the fan. It was stifling in this store. A third copy of the receipt was handed to my mother: "Please go to sales counter downstairs." Down we went, to the back of the shop. It never ceased to amaze me that by the time we arrived at the wooden glass-fronted kiosk, the change was waiting for us. But sometimes, if the tubes were busy, our cylinder dropped into the basket with a clunk and a thud while we waited. The cashier opened the tin, checked my mother's receipt and handed her the correct change, nodding towards a queue at the goods counter. Finally, she received her elastic, wrapped in a paper bag. This process, which had taken at least ten minutes, was repeated in Apothecaries, next door, while my mother searched for her favourite Pond's face cream.

"Now I need to go to the Pettah. Daddy needs some new vests and handkerchiefs. It shouldn't take long." My heart sank. We walked out of the shade, back into bright, glaring sun, crows cawing from telegraph posts, towards a patient Peter, where the lace-selling lady accosted us once again as we climbed into the now broiling car. Off we went to downtown Pettah, across bumpy tram lines, with Peter avoiding bullock carts, over-laden fume-belching buses, pedestrians, mangy pie-dogs, bicycles and scrawny cows, wandering around, nosing at rubbish piles. The Pettah was always crowded and being close to the harbour, it was dirty and smelly. Here, parking was scarce. "Please drop us on this corner, Peter. Be back here in half an hour." She looked at her watch, so did he. Out we climbed again, crowds closing around us.

I tried to keep up with her. I couldn't believe my mother enjoyed this place any more than I did. Stalls spilled from open shop fronts onto the pavements themselves, every type of goods available. Watches, shoes, hats, vests, shirts, then cottons, satins, rayons, checks and stripes, every type of colour, bolt after bolt of cloth, plastics, bowls, plates, mops, brushes, spoons, knives, tyres, fans, transistors, on and on, everything one could possibly need. There were raised voices, hawking, spitting, streams of betel juice squirting onto the pavement in front of us, making us dodge, shift from side to side, dark skins, flashing smiles, people squeezing close, pushing, music blaring Indian music from each shop front, smells of spices, frying, heat, cow dung. I lost sight of my mother as she pushed ahead in the crowd, the stream of shoppers closing in after her, the top of my head only elbow height. "Mummy," I called, scared, overcome by exhausting sensations, expecting to be forgotten in this exotic human morass, whilst all the time the strong sun rays beat down relentlessly, endlessly.

Chapter 20

My Own Baby

Jocelyn often wore her dark glasses in the house. After some time I realised it was because she had been crying. When she took them off, I noticed her eyes were red. I never knew the reasons but I tried to keep out of her way.

One day my father searched me out in my room. "Why have you been rude to your mother?" I was standing by the window, looking out. He stood, legs apart, dressed in his white shirt and shorts, just back from the office, arms across his chest, waiting for me to reply. I couldn't say what was on my mind, the words which were screaming inside me, going around and around my head. He repeated his question. I stood mute, no breath inside me, determined not to cry. Again he repeated his question. Silence. I couldn't say the words. *She isn't my mother, she isn't my mother.* Around and around they went and I stubbornly refused to answer him. I was too young to explain to him how unhappy and angry I was. I missed my real mother – she was never referred to or spoken about – and I missed Nicola. I was angry, a difficult child. I was never hugged. No one ever told me they loved me, that I had done well. The only time my father came close was when he gave me a kiss goodnight.

I so longed for a swinging cradle with a doll in it.

My sixth birthday was coming near. Each time we drove under the banyan tree which had spread its roots so wide that the road passed through them, I squeezed my eyes shut, fervently wishing for my doll. My father had told me wishes dreamed about under this special tree, close to the temple, always came true. The day arrived. I was led to the enclosed balcony next to my room, where a sheet was draped over a high object. My heart began to beat more quickly. Rushing towards the sheet, I pulled it off and there, to my joy, was a swinging cradle with a girl doll lying inside. My wish had come true.

I picked her up, cradling her in my arms. She was my very own. She was so pretty, with her blue eyes which opened and closed when I moved her, along with a gentle cry: "Maaa, maaa." She had long blonde hair. She wore a pretty liberty print dress with lace around the neck and poppers at the back, so I could easily undress her. She wore a nappy with fasteners, had a tiny hole in between her legs and came with her own milk bottle. I immediately fell in love with her, christened her Susanna and put her back to sleep under her sheets. But these were no ordinary sheets. My mother had hand-sewn pretty flowers around the edges of the sheets and pillowcase. I treasured them and Susanna, who seemed to fill an aching void inside me.

Chapter 21

The Hill School

I outgrew my nursery school, because aged seven, in 1952, it was decided I would go up to the Hill School, in Nuwara Eliya. This was far away, up in the mountains, where the tea grew. Initially, I had been sent to the International School in Colombo, not far from where we lived. Each day the teachers missed me from class. Searching, they found me standing in a corner, in a corridor, facing inwards, quietly crying, refusing to talk to anyone or join in with school-time activities. The rush and tumble, noise and big groups of strange children must all have been too much for me. Perhaps I got lost in the large school grounds. I was taken away after a week.

Why a boarding school far away in the hills was the answer, I don't know. Perhaps there was no other option and many of my parents' friends were sending their children to this school. We had no choice in those days, we just did what we were told.

So, for days my father had been making me practise doing up my tie, standing me in front of the mirror so I could learn to do it, ensuring the ends were the correct length. He was a stickler for doing things correctly and became angry with me if I got it wrong. "Watch me," he ordered, as he slowly tied his tie. I stood meekly then, practising this new skill while his beady brown eyes watched. I don't remember him ever laughing with me, joking. Life was a serious business. I had brand new clothes – white shirt, grey pleated skirt with shoulder straps and this wretched tie. White socks with leather-soled shiny black shoes completed my uniform. These soles made me slip on the smooth floor tiles so my father took me to the gravelled driveway and showed me how to rub my feet hard on the gritty stones.

A new brown trunk, J.J. SHATTOCK stencilled in white at both ends, had been standing for some time in my bedroom. Each time I looked at it, I felt sick with apprehension. Slowly it filled with a spare skirt, shirts, games kit, sweaters, shoes. I didn't want to say goodbye to Noeline, to leave my home and go off into the unknown.

My toy farm was on the flat earth behind the garage, complete with a farmhouse, haystacks, metal cows, horses, pigs, fences. I had made the houses and haystacks from a plaster of Paris kit, painting them the appropriate colours. Squatting on my heels, each morning I was lost to the world, reorganising my farm, playing with the fences, changing the shape of the fields while brushing away the large red ants which seemed to have a route through the farmyard. They stung if they found bare skin. I picked flowers to decorate the farm garden, clipped off some thick grass stems to feed the cows. Sadly, I packed it all away into a box.

Finally the day arrived. Five o'clock. The train left at seven. Still dark. Noeline woke me. I looked around my familiar room before climbing out of bed, washing and slowly putting on my new clothes. Hot, humid air pressed against my unaccustomed long shirt sleeves, making prickles of sweat run down my arms. For the last time Noeline brushed my thick, dark hair, now cut into a bob. She fixed in a slide to keep the hair out of my eyes. I was terrified. My stomach clenched into a knot; my heart squeezed with emotion, made it hard to breathe. Noeline looked me in the eyes: "Be a good girl. I shall be thinking of you."

While the house boy lifted the trunk, putting it into the car boot, I stood on the gravel, scraping my feet, saying goodbye to my home. Noeline embraced me. She was leaving for a new job, but I didn't know that and was hoping to have her to myself for the next holiday. "I shall miss you, Judy. I shall think of you every day." Could this be happening again – farewells to people I loved?

We set off for the twenty-minute drive to the Fort railway station. Inside my head I said goodbye to the familiar landmarks. My favourite was shady Bullers Road, with Queens Club where I drank iced fresh lime soda in the evenings; the racecourse where we walked in the mornings. Would I ever see them again?

The station was a hubbub – chaotic, noisy, full of pushing bodies, strong smells of spicy food, vendors selling tea, men hawking and spitting, porters running forwards, offering their services. A white face meant a good tip. The porter, wheeling my trunk before him, forced the crowds to part. My father and Jocelyn followed, with me tightly holding his hand.

"This way, master. Missy going to school?" Obsequious, our porter signalled towards the correct platform, deftly pushing people out of his way. He knew where all the white boys and girls were going. To Udarata Manike, the upcountry express train, towering beside the platform, its doors open, a giant, dirty red-brown, waiting to gobble us up. Huddles of other families were standing around, their grey-uniformed children looking in all directions, trying to recognise a familiar face in the scrum. I didn't know anyone. I gripped my father's hand more firmly. Jocelyn pulled out her handkerchief releasing a waft of her favourite lavender toilet water, the perfume so at odds in this tropical miasma.

We found the teacher in charge. Introducing herself, she checked her list. "Hello, Judy Jane, your seat is over there," she said, pointing towards the next compartment. "Five minutes until the train leaves. Why not put your bags in before you say your goodbyes?" Climbing up the high steps, helped by my father, we found the seat where he put my holdall beside me. Jocelyn waited on the platform. Anxious parents were walking up and down the carriage, bumping into the sides of the seats, lifting bags onto the rack. Some children were crying, others chattering. "I'll say goodbye now, darling, and wait outside with Mummy until the train leaves. Have a safe journey. I shall write soon." He gave me a big hug and a kiss. "I shall stand outside this window so you can see us. Miss Briggs wants us to get off once you are settled, in case the train leaves with us." I sat still on the hard, slippery seat, my body rigid, looking through the window, watching as my father stepped off the train. He walked back towards where I was staring, motionless, frozen in the moment; and putting his arm around Jocelyn's shoulders, he smiled and mouthed, "Goodbye, darling."

He looked strong, handsome, his thick, dark hair combed off his face, arms crossed; a rock in the midst of a platform of moving, swirling bodies. He was dressed for the office – white shirt and shorts, knee-high white socks, brown laced-up shoes. Jocelyn, beside him in her pretty cotton sundress, turned towards me, smiling, as they spoke to each other. I tried to etch the picture into my mind forever.

The train gave a loud whistle, doors slammed and Miss Briggs asked everyone to sit in their places. I was trying not to cry. There was a lurch, a hissing of steam, then slowly the train began to move. Jumping up I pressed my face to the window. The girl next to me was doing the same. My father stood resolutely, legs braced, waving as we moved away. He got smaller and smaller and smaller, finally disappearing as the train rounded a bend.

Chapter 22

Eva

I sat down. The girl sitting next to me had bright brown eyes, dark curly hair, a cheeky smile. "Hello, my name is Eva. What is yours?" And that was how I made my first friend.

This was to be a seven-hour journey. The fact that it was through some of the most dramatic scenery in the world was lost on us all. The low country of coconuts and lush paddy fields soon gave way to distant hills, trees, rivers. Each station had its name written in English, Singhalese and Tamil script with the height above sea level written in numbers underneath. Somewhere on the platform stood a tall pole, marked in feet, with a red line noting the level to which the water reached at the latest flood. Sometimes these marks were above the top of the station roof. As we neared Kandy, the ancient capital of the Kandyan kings, strategically built amongst hills at 1500 feet, the train slowed, grinding its way up the incline with smut-laden smoke belching from the engine's funnel. Smut got everywhere – in our eyes, our clothes, even on the outside of tins of condensed milk some of us were allowed to have. There were two small holes in the top of the tin and we would suck this delicious sweetness down to the last, sticky drop. Unforgettable.

Often the train stopped completely. Once a man had been run over. The delay seemed to last forever, all the passengers, except us, climbing out to go and look. We weren't even allowed to put our heads out of the windows, although we were fascinated, trying to sneak a view. Sometimes the whole train slithered backwards, the brakes squeaking, grinding, unable to hold the immense weight on the slope. We all cheered, hoping we would be going back to Colombo. Then our driver tried to start. Hissing, whooshing, more thick black smoke from the funnel, our train clanked and jerked forwards, only to slide back. More cheers from us inside, the boys leaning out shouting, "Colombo here we come!" When success came on the third attempt, there were more cheers from us all, accepting our fate. At Kandy, a second engine was attached, as from here to Nanu Oya, the climb became even steeper.

We went through tunnels, crossing rocky ravines, their sides steep and sheer, where, if I put my head right out of the window, I could see and hear water tumbling far below. "Keep your hands inside the windows and stop throwing things," said Miss Briggs as the boys began to relax, getting noisy and silly, throwing pieces of paper at each other and at the small ceiling fans, protected by once white frames.

Finally, at our destination, Nanu Oya, we clambered out, stretching our legs. Eva and I were now inseparable, staying close to each other. It was cool. The air smelled fresh after the enclosed compartment. Two o'clock in the afternoon. We needed our coats. We were shepherded, in an orderly line, onto a waiting bus, THE HILL SCHOOL painted in white letters on the side. Hard wooden seats offered no comfort but we were all too engrossed in finding a space close to newly made friends. Another long journey of an hour followed, our bus straining around every hairpin bend, roads winding steeper and steeper, past high jungle-clad slopes with sheer drops from the edge causing us to gasp with fear. We passed more tea fields until we reached Nuwara Eliya, at 6,000 feet. Here the climate was just like England – rain, mists, wind.

Our school stood on the far side of the lake from the town, a low white building dwarfed by a large hill. The entrance drive curved around the bottom playing field, up into the playground. Finally our nearly nine-hour journey was at an end.

Chapter 23

Miss Plum

My dormitory, for the youngest girls, was called Fry. Named after famous women – Fry, Melba, Thorndike, Curie, Pavlova, Bronte, Cavell, Nightingale – the dormitory names are still on the tip of my tongue, remembered like an old ditty.

As I write I can see the long corridor leading from Fry to the rest of the dormitory block, where double doors, painted brown with the name on the outside, opened onto bare floor on which stood black metal beds, each with its own locker. As we grew older and moved up the school the dormitories became smaller, five or six girls in each room. At a corner stood a small enclosed courtyard, which caught the sun at midday. Here we grew cress seeds on old pieces of towel, sheltered between plant pots. Each morning we found fat, long slimy slugs, satiated, sliding across the concrete floor, leaving sticky trails behind.

Fry was a single-storey long wooden block, seven beds down the side walls, facing each other. Our burgher matron, Miss Plum, slept in a small room between us and the bathrooms. We were forbidden to go into her room. Miss Plum had black hair and always wore red lipstick with a woollen sweater and straight skirt. Each week we would line up as she checked our heads for nits and looked into our ears to see whether they were clean. She was strict but she must have been loving as well, as I remember her clearly, with affection. Our beds were covered with cotton counterpanes. She taught us to pair up, to fold them neatly between us and put them on our lockers for the night. The reverse happened in the mornings. Our possessions were put into our wooden lockers beside our metal beds. On the top of my locker I had a photo of my father on one side and Jocelyn on the other, in a folding blue leather frame. It was my most treasured possession.

Outside our dormitory was a grassy bank overlooking the large playing field with woods on the far side. A septic tank with a rail around its concrete top stood away from this bank. It was the perfect spot to go for a little peace. Standing there, looking over the green playing field, towards the lake, to the right, I could see mountains silhouetted against the sky. I was so terribly homesick I imagined Colombo behind those hills. At that time of day when the sun was low and we were all tired, I would stand there, thinking about my father, my home, the swimming pool I loved so much. The pain was in the pit of my belly – strong, consuming.

I was an extremely unhappy child, probably difficult to handle and headstrong. I also talked too much. It turned out that I was quite clever in class. One year I skipped a whole year, and proved to be good at sports, so my peer group probably disliked me. Girls don't like girls who are good at things.

At this school, in 1952, we were called by our surnames. My friend Eva was E. Beck and I was J.J. Shattock, often shortened to J.J. The boys were called only by their surnames. The three Hooper boys were Hooper major, Hooper minor and Hooper minimus. On school lists or photographs it would be ma, mi, min.

The first day back at school was a day off to enable us to become acclimatised to the altitude. Nearly half of the pupils lived on tea or rubber estates, from high and low country, their names rolling off the tongue... Dickoya, Dimbula, Uva, Pusselawa, Passara and Bogawantalawa, which was where my father's great uncle had planted. Some came from estates close to Galle in the south and some from Kandy, where they caught the convoy train as it ground into the station. If they were too remote, they would have to have been brought by car to school.

We all had one thing in common. We were a long way from 'home', as England was called, far from our families of grandparents, uncles, aunts, cousins, siblings, who had been sent back to senior school. In the early fifties telephones were used for emergencies so letters were the easiest way of communication. Life on a tea estate could be lonely for a child with no siblings, but once at school, friendships were formed. Many of these have lasted into our adult lives.

Chapter 24

Mr Jobson

Each Sunday, after church, we went to our classrooms to 'write home'. We had to write as far as a ruled line had been drawn, two thirds of the way down the page. The teacher would check that this had been done before we could leave the room to go and play. For me it began a lifetime's habit, a discipline which brought many rewards. My father wrote to me every week. These letters transported me back home, to security and love, which I missed. I so looked forward to these snippets of news, even though, sometimes, my pleasure was tinged with annoyance. If I had made a spelling mistake, he would write, "You have spelt banana incorrectly. In your next letter please write it out ten times." He was a stickler for doing everything properly.

From the first day we were taught Latin and French, English, history and maths. Our class windows looked out onto the playground on one side, the lower field on the other. They were light and airy – white walls, concrete floor, one wall completely taken up with a blackboard. Our chairs scraped each time someone moved and the boys were always leaning back, swinging on the chair's back legs, laughing, joking, making a noise. Our class door opened onto a covered way leading to the other classes and the lavatory block. It was always smelly in there, damp, with graffiti on the wall, the water in the dirty hand basin cold. The boys seemed to have more problems with concentrating than us girls, always moving, joking, asking to leave the room.

Two male teachers, Mr Knight and Mr Jobson, wore their black graduation gowns, walking from class to class, carrying piles of books. 'Jobey', as we nicknamed him, was terrifying. By class four we had moved to around the corner where the corridor was on two sides of the classroom. Jobey was our maths teacher. As we heard his footsteps cross the playground, my heart began to beat wildly and we rushed to our desks, pencils and paper ready. The first mental arithmetic question came at the first window, the next at the second, until he was at the door with another question. Beside his desk, each movement was accompanied by another question. Heads bowed and utter silence reigned as all fourteen of us, resigned to what may happen, scribbled frantically. Finally, by number ten, the last, he was sitting down. We swapped papers with the person adjacent to us, Jobey read out the answers, and we ticked those correct and swapped papers back. The worst part of the day began. "Those with one wrong, stand up." Chairs scraped. "Those with two wrong, stand on your chair." We hardly dared move. "Those with three wrong, stand on your desk." Poor Robin Baxter found these questions impossible. Jobey would grab him by the hair and bang his head against the wall to the rhythm of his chanting, "Baxter, Baxter, get them right, do you understand?"

To this day I am bad at figures. My eyes glaze over at

the sight of numbers and I count on my fingers. Jobey has a lot to answer for.

Mr Knight obviously loved the booze, although we were too young to understand why we would find graphic drawings on our blackboard in the mornings. Often he opened the girl's bathroom door, 'by mistake', when we were all piled into the hot, steamy water. We had communal baths in those days.

The four school houses had very patriotic names – George, Andrew, David, Patrick. We collected class and games points towards our house winning the cup. Mr Knight ran George house: "If George wins this year, I shall eat my hat." George won. It was around the school in a trice: "Mr Knight is going to eat his hat!" We had our end of term supper when house notices were read and the house cup was presented. Anticipation rose and amidst cheers and shouts, he ate the whole pastry replica of a hat. He was very rotund.

Chapter 25

Films, Scottish Dancing and the Woods

Each morning assembly was in the main hall. We sang a hymn and listened to prayers, after which the headmaster, Mr Spurrier, would address us, usually about plans, activities, typical school notices. He was a fair man, much respected by us all. But one day there was a scandal. As we grew older many of us developed strong crushes on the boys, and I am sure, they with us. We would send sweeties to our 'beloved' via a third party, giggling, hiding to watch the handover. With my friends standing at the top of the corridor behind the door frame, we tried to catch a glimpse of their naked bodies as they dashed for their showers.

Mr Spurrier spoke severely to us this particular morning. "Last night some girls were caught down in the boys' dormitories. Please stand up anyone who was involved." You could have heard a pin drop in that large room. Everyone was holding their breath, cautiously looking around at the rows of one hundred and twenty other cross-legged pupils. The silence became intense, long. Eventually two girls, more senior than myself at that time, stood up. Later, they must have been reprimanded and the boys as well. Boys were beaten on the backside. We often saw them lined up outside the study. We walked quickly past. Girls had their palms hit with a cane.

The hall was used for everything, but best of all was film nights on Fridays. Stickjaw was a particularly delicious, hard, gritty square of flapjack, which nearly broke your teeth. We were allowed to take a piece or two, if we were lucky, into the hall after supper, to eat while we sat on the dusty wooden floor to watch the film. They were Pathé news reels, the old black and white movies.

One of the masters worked the projector. "Nine, eight, seven, six…" we all chanted together, full of anticipation as the film spool unwound at the start of the film. Lights went on when the spool was changed, then once again we were plunged into darkness, and Tarzan continued swinging his way through the jungle. Johnny Weissmuller – we loved him. What a physique! The boys were in love with Jane, with her long hair and skimpy dress.

The Hill School provided us with plenty of activities. We had Scottish dancing evenings. We would gather in the hall and Miss McKinnon would carry her old gramophone, put it on the stage, wind it up, take out her supply of black plastic records kept in their paper covers and place the shiny record head with its sharp needle onto the record. She clapped her hands for silence and asked us to make up pairs.

We learned the Eightsome Reel and the Dashing White Sergeant, but how I loved Strip the Willow. Lined up facing each other, the music started. There was a wail of the bagpipes and the rhythm began. Off we went, the first pair dancing small steps facing our partner, then linking arms, swinging around, then swinging each person around down the line, coming back to our partner in the middle. Us girls swung the boys around, trying hard to get them off balance; then the boys swung the girls. The other dancers would cheer and clap, awaiting their turn. We checked the line to see whether we may have the chance to dance with our particular boy of the moment. It was exhilarating, fun, wild.

Sundays, when the weather was cloudy or drizzly, we had to walk around the lake in crocodile formation. It was a long walk, starting past the extensive beds of white arum lilies which grew at the water's edge. Beautifully, naturally arranged, white as far as the eye could see, year in, year out, they were always there. We'd continue around to the end where the water gushed away under a bridge, down a small hill to the far side where straggly evergreen firs grew, protecting English-style houses dotted over the hillside. Above them were tea fields, smooth, green, the cut-off point where natural mountain jungle took over from tea, clearly visible. Now, dragging our heels, we went past the racecourse and sometimes into Victoria Park, out through the second gate, slowly down the shortcut, under the mimosa trees and back up the drive.

With relief we hung up our coats, took off our boots and went to our dormitories where we had our weekly bath. Two or three in together. We seemed to be covered in black wriggly leeches; round our ankles, on our legs and arms. "Don't pull them off," said Miss Plum. "Their heads will stay inside and they become messy. Use the soap." So we soaped these horrid things until they wriggled a bit more then fell into the water. Sometimes we had to pull them off. For weeks the spot where their heads were would itch and itch, sometimes becoming filled with pus, usually leaving a small scar.

When the weather was sunny we were allowed up into the woods to run around and play games. I seem to remember the whole school went, but perhaps it was just the juniors. The path started behind the dining room. It was steep and cut into the red earth with slippery, uneven steps. No hand rail. We passed the passion fruit creeper with its beautiful purple flower with a cross in the middle. Sometimes we picked the hard round fruits. Then up past the shallow quarry to the left of the path until we reached the top where grass grew. This was our base, where the teacher in charge would sit and we'd pile our coats. Then we were allowed to go off, usually in pairs, along the paths. The boys were always in gangs, often ambushing the girls, jumping out at them. We were forbidden to go onto the tarmac road at the back of the woods. On special days, we made a small fire, carefully supervised by the scout master. We broke twigs from a tree, cleaned off the bark and wound a thick, gloopy cheese mixture around our sticks, before cooking them over the fire. Impatiently, we held these twigs over the embers, turning them to cook them evenly, scarcely being able to wait to eat these hot, cheese dreams.

Break time could not come quickly enough. Scrambling out into the playground, we ran round to the back of the classrooms to bag the best spot for marble playing. We had dug small holes in the red clay earth where the compacted surface made perfect runs around the nasturtium beds where bright orange and yellow flowers blew in the breeze. I had a cloth bag, tied with string, filled with my marble collection. It had become very heavy. We swapped these coloured glass balls with a passion. The big ones were worth two, sometimes three of the smaller ones. We played to win. It was cut-throat.

Break-time games went in phases. Next term it was skipping. I badgered my parents until they bought me a rope. Mine was the best. I have it still, J.J. Shattock scratched on the wooden handles. It has ball bearings in the top to enable the rope to swing around smoothly. Each break we would practise jumping backwards, forwards, arms crossed, uncrossed and, most difficult of all, doubles. Two turns before the feet landed back onto the ground. I became school doubles champion, notching up one hundred and twenty before tripping up! Sometimes during break two of us would hold the rope, swinging it around together, allowing one of our group to jump while we chanted, "Strawberry, raspberry, apple jam tart, tell me the name of your sweetheart. A, B, C," and so on. We tried not to tell who we had a crush on. We would giggle, keep it a secret. So we guessed, making sure the girl jumping tripped and stopped, amidst laughs, and when she blushed we called out names, until she blushed more.

Chapter 26

The Dining Room

At mealtimes, in the large, dark dining room, sitting at tables of sixteen, boys in a row, girls in a row, we were fed typical English fare – soup, meat and overcooked cabbage. Servants dressed in white uniforms placed filled plates in front of us. The small dining room behind the stage contained the pig's table where the offenders who were considered to have disgusting table manners sat with a mirror propped up in front of them. Usually they were the most annoying and noisy boys in school, looking extremely embarrassed, uncomfortable. I wonder whether they remember being so openly humiliated and learned to improve their manners?

The dining room had another use. This was for Corrections in Games Time or CGT, which happened always on Friday afternoons. Even now the thought of those CGT sessions brings dread into my heart. I loved any sort of sport and obviously I was rather a noisy child, so I had to miss games in order to write lines, such as 'Empty vessels make most noise', or, another favourite, 'Speech is silver, silence is golden.' I sat there fuming, scribbling away, a thousand lines each time, thinking it was ridiculous having to behave, longing to be outside in the air.

One afternoon the tedium was lightened. One boy

whose name I can't remember – he wasn't very old and was quite slight in stature – had obviously annoyed Mr Knight. "Come here," he said to this unfortunate boy. Slowly he went up to him, fearing the worst. Mr Knight was standing beside the window. A few words were exchanged, then suddenly Mr Knight bent down and, holding the boy by his legs and back, he swung him up into the air, through the open window. He stood there, his back to us, holding this boy in mid-air, one hand on each foot, swinging him. We were shocked into utter silence. "This will teach you a lesson," said this perverted master and he let go, dropping the boy onto the ground outside.

Sundays, out came our grey jackets. At mealtimes we sat at tables of twelve. Six boys in a row, then six girls. The room was always noisy, the windows wide open, the food English and substantial. First we had soup. The worst was slimy green leek soup. It truly slithered down the throat like a living being. It took me many years to even try to eat soup after the Hill School cuisine. The main course was meat or fish, then delicious puddings. Our absolute favourite was Floating Islands. It must have been a blancmange base with cream dolloped on the top. We all loved it. If we wanted a second helping, we sat with our right fist on the table with our thumb sticking up. We tried to catch the eye of the waiter, and piled our left hand on top of our right, for extra emphasis.

The boys would become very noisy and jump up and down until a master came to quieten them. There seemed to have been a strong fascination between Alan Smith and myself. Both of us had stored a row of pins in our jacket pocket, and for some reason, we spent the entire mealtime pricking each other's arms. It only happened on Sundays.

Then it was off to church in Hotchkiss, the bus converted from a leaf lorry. Wide mesh now enclosed the space at the back which was originally designed to carry sacks of freshly plucked tea leaf from field to factory. Long wooden seats had been fixed to both sides. Climbing in, we jostled for places at the back, where we could look out, feel the air rushing past our faces. Off we went down the drive, turning right past the tennis court under the overhanging mimosa trees, past the racecourse and the entrance where the horses had their stables, up a narrow, twisty, steep hill to Holy Trinity Church.

Once there we walked in twos, up the gravel path, past the graves. Many of the headstones carried names of young English children who had died of fevers, of women who had died young, like my mother, and were buried there, far from home. The path went under the shady albizzia tree, which blossomed with spectacular feathery flowers, small and pink. If these were in reach, we stretched up to pick a few delicate, fragrant blooms, storing them in our prayer books to press them. Once seated in the narrow pews, when the sermon was too long, our attention lost, we took out our prayer books to swap pieces of silver paper, also stored between the pages. These were multicoloured, patterned chocolate wrappers, which we had saved from our sweetie supply. We had rubbed them hard on a firm surface with the back of a finger nail until each piece was quite flat, making the patterns sparkle.

Chapter 27

Exeat Weekend

My parents had undertaken the long six-hour drive up country, through the Ramboda pass, to visit me for exeat weekend. This happened once a term. They stayed at the four-storey Grand Hotel, with its formal front garden and long, echoing corridors, covered with slippery coir matting. High-ceilinged rooms opened off these corridors, with a sitting room and a bedroom complete with high wooden beds, laden with blankets. It was cold at night. The bathroom was always cold and damp with mosquitoes hiding in the loo, each window sporting discoloured nylon half-nets, hanging disconsolately, keeping the world at bay. Once we turned on the hot tap, the room quickly filled with steam, misting the mirror and the tiles, seeping into our bedroom.

Many of my friends' parents stayed there. Gangs of us children raced along corridors, released from routine, sliding, shouting, playing table tennis in the games room, looking inside the hotel shops. At tea time we sat in the garden, feasting on scones, cream and cakes. They also came to church, although we weren't allowed to sit with our families. By now we were meant to have learned to sit quietly and to listen to the vicar during his sermon, but instead we were leaning towards each other, pointing, whispering and swapping silver papers.

"I shall never come to visit you again," my father said. He was angry, very stern. "You simply must learn to sit still in church." I can hear his words today and still feel the fear. Was he serious? Would he never, ever come to visit me at school again?

For me, the best part of school was games time. Miss Redhouse, with her long grey pleated skirts teamed with a white blouse, inspired and encouraged us all. I promised myself I would be just like her when I grew up. Hockey was played on the big games field where one set of goal posts stood at the wooded end, the other below the school buildings. I was a big, well-covered child; I loved sweet puddings, scrunchy fudge, condensed milk. So I was put as goalie, my legs covered by huge pads. I hated standing still, waiting for the hard, red ball to come at speed, straight towards me. I was terrified. I don't know what happened – perhaps someone noticed I was no good in goal and could run fast, because the next thing I knew I was playing on the forward line. Running up and down, on the left wing, I came to life. Exhilarated, freed from restricting pads, keeping up with the forwards, watching carefully, I determined we should score as many goals as possible.

The thought of holidays kept all of us going. We made end-of-term worms, drawing circles on paper, colouring in each segment, writing the date in the middle, taking great pleasure in cutting off each section at the end of another long day. "Only three days to go," we would shout, running along the corridors.

Holidays were joyous affairs, starting with the bus drive down to Nanu Oya, transferring for the long, slow train journey back. This was helped by our school picnic packets of thick bread, eggs and bananas, all wrapped in greaseproof paper. We grabbed seats with our friends, sang and chanted off the names of each station we went through and worked out how many hours were left until we arrived at the Fort station. Passing Bible Rock, such a big, square landmark, we watched mountains give way to enormous, spreading, creeper-covered trees. Then the scary bridges again, rivers, and finally, paddy fields with clumps of coconut palms under which stood houses thatched with coconut fronds, which had been soaked and dried before being woven into flat mats. Colombo was hot and humid. Our parents were happy to welcome us home.

Chapter 28

No. 10 Jawatta Road

During the last term my parents had moved house to the top end, on the left of Jawatta Avenue, having decided it was too dark and gloomy down the end of the avenue. Number 10 Jawatta Road was next to Minster, our first house, on the opposite side of the avenue. A solid two-storey house, it had two entrance gates, one of which opened onto the main road, the other onto the avenue. Bougainvillea tumbled over the walls, along with my favourite quisqualis creeper, with its drooping pink blooms and heady perfume. In one corner stood the vibrant orange peacock-flower tree, while close by dove orchids grew up the trunk of a cassia. A grass lawn was bordered by the drive.

My bedroom overlooked the servants' quarters. I was forbidden to go there so would watch proceedings from my window, fascinated. The podian, a young boy of about sixteen, who was general dogsbody, spent all morning grinding spices by hand, using a solid flat piece of granite and rolling pestle. Apart from him, we had a cook, a house boy who cleaned the house and served at table and a garden coolie. I could smell the strong beedi cigarettes they smoked, heard the laughter and chatter and music from their radio and longed to join in the fun they seemed to be having.

Mealtimes were formal affairs, sitting at our long, highly polished, dark wooden table, the places laid with crisp white embroidered linen. Water filled glass finger bowls, in which perfumed jasmine flowers, fragrant lime leaf or pink quisqualis blooms floated, so we could rinse our fingers after eating juicy mangoes. Looking out through French windows at the side, where the bird bath stood, we watched brightly coloured sunbirds flit in and out of their cover in the bright yellow hanging allamanda creeper, noisy Seven Sisters birds, in a group, foraging under the hedge.

Munianday waited discreetly behind the stairs for my stepmother to ring the little brass bell. With a swish of his sarong and quiet thud of bare feet, he collected the used plates and brought the next course while we sat under the fan, being waited upon. It was the tail end of the colonial era, mid-1950s.

I was given a small circular bed as my garden. Edged with stones, it had a tall papaya tree growing in the middle, giving shade to my plants. Snails were a pest and I always wanted pocket money. "I will give you one cent per snail, if you collect them for me. But you have to do it very early in the morning." My father taught me how to manage money. One day he gave me a small accounts book. He showed me how to put my earnings in one column and expenditure in another.

As a result I was up when the morning was cool, when dew was lying on the grass, before the garden coolie had started to sweep the drive. Early enough to hear the horses clip-clopping past, down Jawatta Road. Collecting my bucket from the garage I poked about all the crevices in the walls, under the creepers, picking up stones, pulling large grey-brown snails out of their hiding places and into my bucket. Their mantles were slimy and revolting and the bucket became heavy. I had to count them then take them to the garden coolie who would pour boiling water over them to kill them. The next morning there seemed to be just as many snails, but my father paid up, and I saved up for my favourite books

Each night the house boy came upstairs with the flit gun. This metal contraption was filled with DDT. A pump like that for a bicycle allowed the liquid to be sprayed everywhere. I heard him coming, listening as he went to each room in turn, pumping hard – poosh, poosh, poosh. The flit gun clicked as Muniandy pulled back the plunger, increasing the pressure. The smell was horrid. I would run away, covering my nose. He bent to spray under the beds, behind the chest, inside the cupboards. Just a tiny crack of darkness was a haven for malaria-carrying mosquitos, safely hiding during daylight. At dusk they emerged, zooming in on our warm skin, just when we were enjoying the cool evening. Mosquito repellent hadn't been invented then. The ceiling fan kept most at bay during the night, but let a foot or elbow become uncovered during sleep and itchy red lumps would be the result. We all suffered; one of the discomforts of our tropical home.

Our garden coolie used Jeyes Fluid to wash out the drains where cockroaches and other unpleasant creatures lived. These primitive, disgusting insects with their shiny brown bodies and long antennas lived everywhere. We stamped on them when they scuttled out from their hiding places, their oozy insides spread on the tiles which had to be wiped away.

Standing in the garden, I watched the garden coolie using a broom to push along the white strong-smelling liquid through the open drains which surrounded our house. Sometimes a polecat was flushed out from the dark area under the front doorstep. Then I would run away, up the stairs to the safety of the veranda. These polecats lived in drains and roofs, sleeping during the day. Often we heard them scratching and moving around above our heads at night. That scared me as well as the thought that, in the dark, someone might climb through my open bedroom window.

A varsacooty came every day to clean the bathrooms. He was a man of low caste who had this menial job. "After your shower, or your bath, Judy, make sure there are no toenail clippings or lengths of hair left in the bathtub," Father said. "Why?" I asked. He looked at me, his eyes fathomless. "It's because of black magic." He was deadly serious. "If one of the servants, or somebody else, has a grudge against you, they will pay the varsacooty to collect these personal scraps. They take them to the voodoo man. He will then put a spell on you." My father terrified me when he was in this mood. He was dark-skinned with black hair. He had thick, bushy eyebrows which he sometimes would pull down until the hairs touched his lips. They quickly sprang back into place. My family often said, "Gary has a touch of the tar brush," inferring there was Singhalese blood in his veins.

Chapter 29

Sarah

We did have a burglar one night. He crawled silently up the wooden staircase. I don't know how he managed to avoid the creaks. The frogs would be making their deafening noise from the other side of the road, in the ponds of the Irrigation Department, and our ceiling fans squeaked slightly, possibly covering the sound of his progress. Gently slithering along the tiled landing, turning left by the bathroom, he stole into my parents' bedroom. They kept their door propped open at night, using a brick covered with cloth as a doorstop. Our burglar was aiming for the far side of the bed, where my mother slept with her handbag under her pillow. It must have been uncomfortable. My father slept like a cat. He woke the instant he heard a strange noise. Sitting up, he said, "Who's there?" Jumping up, the startled burglar ran through the dressing room, across the veranda, and jumping from the second floor onto the drive, he continued down Jawatta Road, quite naked. My father followed him, but he had managed to get away.

We found his clothes in a pile on the floor at the bottom of the stairs. "Why did he undress, Daddy?" I asked, curiously. "Well, with his dark brown skin he would have blended in with the night. His light-coloured sarong would have been too obvious. I heard him, anyway."

The next day my father interviewed all the servants, finally dismissing the new kitchen podian. He had looked cheeky when I secretly watched him from my bedroom window, leaning against a wall, hidden from the cook, smoking a beedi. Upstairs there were no frames or glass windows on the large veranda openings, just tats made from the central stalk of the coconut leaf. These were rolled up during the day, their long strings carefully wound around a side hook. Sometimes we pulled them down to block the sunlight or when the monsoon winds were blowing hard, to keep the heavy rain out. Now, each night, these were bolted to a frame we had made.

Immediately next door, in an almost identical house but with a much bigger garden, lived my friend Sarah. She was the only daughter of much older parents. They had a much-loved golden cocker spaniel who sat beside them every day, while they were served afternoon tea on the lawn. Sarah's bedroom window looked over towards mine. The moment we arrived home we badgered my father to help us with our plan.

We had decided to link our bedrooms with a rope and basket so we could pass messages to each other. My father banged in two staples at the bottom of the black wooden window frame on my side and the same on Sarah's window. Then he bought us a long length of rope together with a ball of string. We had the greatest fun attaching one end to a small stone, throwing it over the wall, rushing next door and up the stairs to let down the string with a weight attached, tying them together, pulling the long one up, passing it through the staples. Repeating the process we finally made a complete loop. We tied a basket onto the rope… finally we were ready. We passed books, notes, dolls, sometimes even food. It was the greatest fun – our lifeline.

We made up a special whistle: "Phewww, phewww, phewww." Sometimes Sarah's house boy looked out of the window. "Missy out," he would say, or "Missy swimming."

Sarah came to the window one day. "Are you going to the pool?" she asked. "No, I have to go for a dress fitting," I shouted. We had matching party dresses, sleeveless and white with tiny red spots, red trim and bows around waist and hem. "When will you be back?" she said. "Come over after rest time and we can get the play ready," I answered. In the heat of the afternoon I climbed the jam tree, still in flower, not yet ready to give up its fruit, clambering on top of the wall, then pausing before dropping down onto her huge, smoothly cut lawn. I ran to her brick-built Wendy house. "You draw the invitations – we are nearly ready for our show. Let's ask the grown-ups next week." Sarah was very artistic and made puppets, which we covered with remnants from her big dressing-up box. We wrote our plays together.

Most nights my parents went out to a party. These were usually business cocktail parties at Queens Club, down the Bullers Road from us, or at the cricket club, past the racecourse, or at the Galle Face Hotel, on the way to the Fort. I sat on my parents' bed, under the fan, watching my stepmother apply her make-up, dab perfume behind her ears, swirl around in front of her mirror and swish out, looking pretty, happy.

"Will you be alright? Mummy has ordered brains for you. Muniandy will bring your supper upstairs." My father was always solicitous but he must have felt bad going out, night after night. I was having a special treat, as brains in white sauce was my absolute favourite. Covered with breadcrumbs, set in a small round dish, piping hot from the oven, I was thrilled. At the corner of the tray was a bowl filled with tinned pears, and joy of joys, a screw-top jar, cold and dripping from the icebox, filled with condensed milk.

The tats were down, my supper finished, and I had my father's pile of yellow weekly editions of *Daily Mirror* newspapers for company. I sat under the fan, close to our fish tank, where two angel fish swam lazily around, reading news from 'home'.

Ratnapura, December 1901.
My grandparents Wedding. Left to Right: Susan Shattock (seated,
nee Bois), Mark Shattock (my great grandparents), Mabel Byrde (my
grand mother, the bride), Mark Shattock (my grandfather, the groom)
and William Byrde (my great uncle – to the groom's right).

Norfolk, 1930.
Anne, Jean (my mother), Granny Gates and Michael.

Firgrove, Ash Vale, 1941.
My parents Wedding. Back row Left to Right: Uncle Michael,
Uncle Henry (Shattock), Sydney Barrington Gates ('Grandpa').
Front row Left to Right: Granny Burns (my father's mother),
my parents: Edgar and Jean, and Granny Gates.

Firgrove, Ash Vale, 1948.
Nicola, my mother and myself,
just before we left for Colombo.

Galle Face hotel,1948.
Nicola, myself and our ayah.

Beach road, 1949.
Nicola, my mother Jean and myself.

Minster garden, 1950.
Myself, my father and Nicola,
on the day he married Jocelyn.

Nicola and myself dressing up in Minster garden.

House servants in front of Abbotsford, Jawatta Road.

The Gully Gully man with his cobra.

Exeat from the Hill School, myself aged about 6, tea bushes behind.

My handsome father, Edgar, who loved his camera.

Passekudah Estate, Manager's bungalow

Bentota
Weekend bungalow on 'the spit'.

Eva's tenth birthday.
Back row Left to Right: Daphne, Valerie, Tessa, Patty, Elizabeth.
Front row Left to Right: Carol, Eva, Vanessa, myself, Cheryl, Nicky.

*Myself, with friend Sarah from next door,
in our matching party dresses.*

*Jocelyn and myself,
before I left for school in England.*

Chapter 30

Growing Up

"Mummy, what is a prostitute?" An innocent question from me next morning, after breakfast. I hadn't been able to understand why these women were in trouble. The *Daily Mirror* was full of pictures of women in leather coats and high heels, with long, straggly hair, eyes heavily made up, showing plenty of leg.

She looked at me, then looked away, suddenly becoming busy, walking out of the room without answering me. Next day, when he returned from the office after tea, my father said, "You asked your mother about prostitutes yesterday?" He wasn't angry but had chosen the right time to speak to me. Jocelyn was not around. For the first time in my life I was aware of a shift in my perception. I had asked a question which my stepmother had been unwilling to answer. The subject had obviously been discussed between them. His answer, "They are women who wait in their doorway until their boyfriends arrive to take them out," didn't really satisfy me. Last night I had read all about these women and that they were doing something illegal. "Have you been reading my papers?" He was smiling. "Yes, I really enjoy them," I said. "Well, keep asking the questions," he replied.

I was growing up.

Sometimes my supper was put on the table downstairs. My reflection in the glass doors, closed now to keep out mosquitoes, looked back at me. It was scary sitting there on my own. Eating quickly, trying not to imagine someone was hiding outside, behind the glass, I would rush upstairs, round the bend past the Swiss wooden cuckoo clock, convinced I was being followed.

We had a system with the electric bell on the veranda. One ring was for Muniandy to come upstairs for us to request him to do something for us, two rings and he arrived with the drinks tray. He unloaded glasses, ice bucket, bottles of Scotch, gin, sweet vermouth and my favourite, passion fruit cordial, from his tray onto the glass trolley. In his other hand he had carried up the cane basket which held dripping ice-cold soda, tonic and ginger ale.

Three rings was for lunch or dinner to be served. We waited for the brass gong to be rung, then the three of us would clatter down the polished wooden stairs.

I hated asking anyone to come upstairs for a simple request, even a glass of water, so I went down into the dark, cool pantry room, where the white mesh-fronted cupboard stood, its four legs in saucers of disinfectant water to keep away the ants.

Once a month we heard the tinkle of a bicycle bell at the gate. "The fudge man!" my father and I would shout in unison as I ran from the lunch table towards the gate to let him in. Smiling, he rested his bicycle under the porch, opening the wooden box which stood on the passenger pillion. And there was the fudge! Oblong packets, piled on top of each other, neatly wrapped in greaseproof paper. Chocolate, vanilla, cashew and coconut, warm, as though they had just been made, but in reality, hot from the sun. Delicious, quite like nothing I have ever tasted since. It melted in your mouth, soft but firm, slightly scrunchy, unforgettable. "What shall we get this week, Daddy?" I would ask, knowing what he would say. "What about cashew nut and vanilla this time?" he'd smile conspiratorially. "Let's get a third one. Chocolate. Don't tell Mummy." He licked his lips in anticipation. We both loved fudge. We went into the cool, dark pantry. My job was to unwrap the greaseproof paper covering the bars, breaking them into bite-sized squares. Two pieces each, then the rest went into a large, glass-stoppered jar which we kept in the store cupboard. It didn't last long. Lying spreadeagled on my bed for my afternoon rest, cooled by the lazy black fan which creaked as the vanes spun around, I savoured the melting sweetness while I read and read. When the house seemed still, I crept downstairs into the pantry to lift the jar lid for another shot of exquisite deliciousness.

Chapter 31

Journey to the East Coast

Passekudah. The name still evokes huge emotion. Rocky headlands protecting the perfect, curved bay, fringed by palms, where endless, shining blue ocean, broken only by white surf hitting the reef, meets the sky. In my mind the beach is always deserted, broken palm fronds, coconut husks and seaweed littering the sand, crabs scuttling to and fro while gulls await the fish shoals.

And that is how it was. Each year, we would pack the car and leave Colombo well before dawn, my mother, father and I. In a fever of excitement I sat in the back of the Morris Minor, squashed by the last-minute bag, the woven cane picnic basket and thermos flasks, my legs sticky on the plastic seat, chin resting on the hard, cool window glass, looking, looking, staring out at awakening life. Already children were walking along the roadside towards school. Girls in immaculate white dresses with black hair – oiled, parted, neatly plaited – tied by colourful ribbons, they walked together, chatting, schoolbooks under their arms. Small boys weighed down with oversized rucksacks hurried behind them, their white shirts spotless, blue shorts showing long, skinny legs. Even during my early years, watching youngsters coming out of humble Kajan-thatched homes, I marvelled as to how their mothers managed to keep their clothes so clean and white.

Traffic was always dense; overloaded buses belching out black nauseous fumes followed each other along our route. 'Hold-your-breath buses' was our nickname for these elderly vehicles, many of which had started their lives in London. Clusters of elegant sari-clad women, male office workers, their trousers and shirts neatly pressed, queued on the dusty verge, patiently waiting for a seat. Each time the bus stopped, we stopped, the road being too narrow to pass safely. Lorries piled high with bananas, coconuts or papaya, made their way to market. Bicycles, usually carrying two people, one balancing on the cross bar, wound in and out of the chaos; bullock carts swayed past, the driver using his big toe to urge his beast forward. Lean and muscled coolie workers, dressed in vests and tied-up sarongs, chewed betel nut, spitting a stream of red juice onto the road beside us as they hurried to their paddy fields. On each corner, sweepers pushed the rubbish into neat piles, while mangy pie-dogs, ribs sticking out, tits hanging loosely, nosed amongst the debris, as Buddhist monks in their saffron-coloured robes quietly picked their way to the bus queue.

Slowly, we left the capital behind, heading out towards the east coast. The road narrowed. Now, in the shade of rain trees, village boutiques were opening, men queuing for hoppers, rice pancakes, tea and beedi cigarettes, which were bought and lit, their acrid fumes drifting into our car. We passed fruit stalls where large bunches of green, yellow or red bananas hung beside the yellow king coconuts. Under the thatched roof, mangoes, limes, pineapples, nobbly soursops and grapefruits were neatly displayed. There was all-encompassing noise. Singhalese music, discordant and plaintive, blared from every small shop. Voices were raised, crows pecking in the dust, cawing, everyone alive, moving with intention towards their workplace.

Our lengthy journey was always accompanied by Radio Ceylon, pouring out heart-wrenching favourites from our car radio: 'Theme from a Summer Place', 'To Know Him is to Love Him', 'Tammy'… one after another, interspersed with advertisements.

It all burns into my consciousness. I absorb music, movement, brilliant colours, people, village smells, and later, jungle sounds; breathing hot, pungent air into my very being. Years later I realised I was as a lover, knowing I had to be separated from my beloved Ceylon to go to school in England, grabbing every eyeful, squeezing every sensation into my devouring mind.

We played car games starting with Bhud Bhud. The first person to spy a saffron-robed Buddhist monk scored a point. Shaven-headed, carrying an umbrella and begging bowl, these monks could be seen everywhere. As the day progressed we moved on to Animal, Mineral and Vegetable, each of us choosing the most obscure, impossible objects for the others to guess.

By early afternoon we were driving through long stretches of jungle, the bumpy tarmac road shimmering in front, a narrow divide between untamed wilderness. Mile after mile of dense greenery, where creepers stretched over trees, with the occasional glimpse of blue plumbago or yellow acacia. No people, just heat blowing into our small car.

"We might see an elephant, Judy. It's very remote here." I searched and searched through the dense undergrowth but never saw a moving creature – it was too hot. Nearing the end of our journey, we slowed down by some road works. A culvert was undergoing repair, the main road barred and closed. A track led round to the left, close to the trees. Pa drove slowly, gently down the rutted slope, reaching the bottom. He stopped, pressed the accelerator and our wheels spun. He tried again, the wheels spun and he swore. We were stuck. Total silence.

Jocelyn wrung her handkerchief, not saying a word. My heart started thumping. I wished Pa hadn't mentioned the elephants. The workmen had long since gone and the afternoon air was rich with vibrating cicadas, trees motionless, the place deserted. My father got out, looked at the loaded Morris whose wheels were submerged in thick, red oozy clay and shook his head. "We are completely stuck. I certainly can't push this car out."

"I'll help, Daddy. Mummy can too, can't you? We can all push." I opened the door, jumped out. But Jocelyn hunched in her seat, sunglasses on, still nervously clutching her handkerchief, rolling it into a ball. "No, it's impossible. The three of us aren't strong enough. Just be patient. Someone will come," she said. "What about the elephants, Daddy? It's not safe here." I was frightened. I could sense Jocelyn's anxiety coming off her in waves. "Don't worry, we shall be alright!" he said.

So we got out the picnic basket and had a cup of tea. The thermos water was tepid by now, but it filled the time. How slowly it passed. Minutes ticked by, then half an hour. I was sure I could smell wild animals. Perhaps we would be here all night? It was getting darker. Now I was really scared, imagining an elephant or perhaps even a leopard charging out at us from the thick trees on either side of the road. We were just a sitting target.

"I can hear a car." My father had the senses of a cat. We sat up expectantly, listening. The reassuring engine sound became louder and louder until a small truck came round the bend. Four young men, laughing, talking, probably on their way to the arrack tavern in the next village, quickly realised our plight and agreed to help. Relief. We climbed out and in a flash we were pushed back on the tarmac; only half an hour to go to our destination.

Chapter 32

Under the Punkah

Finally, after our adventures, we arrived at the entrance to the coconut estate. This was the moment I had been dreaming about. Down the bumpy, rutted track, over the narrow, rattly bridge, beside which Kajan leaves were being soaked in a saltwater pit, their particular acrid odour filling the air. Then, the first glimpse of the famous beach, golden, smooth sand fringed with palms and endless blue sea. My heaven. My stomach churned, my face was hot.

"Daddy, Daddy, we are here. I can't wait to get into the sea." I stuck my head out of the window, sniffing like a dog as we followed the winding, sandy path through rows of tall, graceful palm trunks, to a small clearing. There sat the estate manager's bungalow, square, roofed with coconut thatch, fifty yards from the shore. My excitement knew no bounds.

George Sawtain, the manager, elderly, lean, bowlegged, tanned, inscrutable, followed by the cook, Apu, came out to meet us. Exchanging greetings – my father knew George well – we were shown to our rooms on the left side of the bungalow. My bedroom was dark and cool, with a polished concrete floor, sparsely furnished. Quickly I unpacked my bag, put on my costume and ran down the path between the scrubby hedges, feeling the sandy, gritty warmth under my toes. Gazing out to where a large rock marked the line of the coral reef, I waited for my parents to catch up.

Then I took the first steps through sea so translucent I could notice all the lines and marks on my toes, the water pressing against my legs, cool in the evening. Trailing my fingers in the sea beside me, walking slowly, I savoured the feel of firm sand under my feet, water inching up my body, the sound of wavelets breaking behind me on the shore. At last it was deep enough to dive. Off I went. Hands outstretched, gliding through this welcoming, supportive salt ocean, as free as a fish, kicking, swimming, twisting and turning, shaking off the heat and containment of a whole day's travelling. Later, floating on our backs, we luxuriated in the knowledge that we had a whole week in this paradise.

During my very first visits to Passekudah, a punkah hung just over our heads above the dark-wood dining table. This table-wide, three-feet-deep piece of fringed velvet, attached to a wooden strut, was suspended by narrow ropes from the ceiling. Two thick cords attached to both ends of the strut, then joined together and disappeared through a small hole high in the wall, between us and the kitchen. Squatting on the floor behind this wall was a small podian, whose job it was to pull on the cord back and forth, in order to waft a breeze over us while we ate.

The heat at mealtimes could be sliced with a knife, thick and heavy with no breeze; even the palms looked dejected. Sweat pricked the temples, trickling down our faces, backs, fronts – our whole bodies would be wet. The punkah was vital, although I felt discomforted by the thought of the small boy working so hard. He probably had worked out an easy method to pull the cord without too much effort and enjoyed the small bonus he received.

Breakfasts consisted of mango, papaya, pineapple and tea from a large white pot. George had gone on his rounds so the three of us sat together under the punkah, looking out into the brightness, sun glinting off the sea, planning our day. We'd already had our early-morning swim when the water was cool and calm; our personal pool. My father would relax on the rubber lilo while I swam, pulling him out to sea. When I hoped he was lulled by my endeavours and inattentive, I tried to shake him off. The sand sloped so gently, was so firm underfoot, it was the perfect spot for fun.

Aged eight or nine, I didn't realise that my father was an important visitor. Food was especially prepared. Crab, juicy, succulent prawns, fish, brinjal, egg with poppadums, freshly grated coconut, sambals. Pa loved hot curries. My favourite was yellow dhal – smooth, spicy and rich, and easy to swallow when mixed up with rice and mango chutney. Our tall water glasses dripped onto the wooden table. Sometimes I had lime soda; George and Pa drank beer. Conversation ranged from estate matters, to worries about the workers, to stories from the past. Faded sepia prints of life in the early 1900s hung on the walls behind us, the sea constantly glinting beyond the path, enticing, bewitching. Falling into that welcoming, calm, cool water was balm to the body and soul.

When I was younger, we used to stay at Kalkudah, two miles around the headland from Passekudah Bay. Rest houses were well known in Ceylon, some better than others. They were all built in the most beautiful spots, affording the traveller a friendly welcome, cold beer, superb curry lunch and rooms. Kalkudah Rest House lay on an extensive beach which stretched south, unending, towards the lagoon and Batticaloa. The Kajan-thatched house, as most buildings were in this part of the island, had been built beside a grove of giant trees whose branches overhung the roof, casting welcoming, dappled shade everywhere. These trees were the home to troupes of grey monkeys who swung from branch to branch, mothers nursing young, their tiny arms wrapped around their mothers' bellies. They were always on the move, chattering excitedly, their small beady eyes watching us from the safety of their branches. The braver ones jumped onto the roof with a light thump, their feet skittering on the palm fronds, then onto the sand, coming close if we were not looking, searching for items to eat, small objects to pick up and take away. Nothing could be left lying around. I spent hours standing under the trees watching their antics, counting the babies, searching out the old male who kept a protective eye on his women.

The bathrooms were primitive. If we were lucky, rust-coloured brackish hot water trickled from a central shower head. In the early fifties, flush toilets hadn't reached this part of the world. The loo seat was fixed above a box, which was removable from the outside. A smaller box, full of sand and a small spade, stood by the seat. This sand was to be sprinkled into the 'Thunder Box' after you had finished. "Judy, make sure no one is close by when you visit the bathroom. The varsacooty has to empty the box every day." Poor man. Luckily I never caught him going about his unpleasant daily task!

Chapter 33

Copra

Each visit my father drove the green Morris along the narrow sandy track, which wound its way through acres of palms, their bending grey trunks lining the path, towards the copra-processing sheds, right into the centre of the estate. George met us there, proudly pointing out new planting areas, those which needed more fertiliser or pruning, bringing my father up to date with his day-to-day management. Lee Hedges were his agents, responsible for getting the best copra prices at auction.

Long, narrow sheds with pointed thatched roofs stood in a clearing beside piles of coconuts, where a well-muscled worker, dressed only in his loin cloth, his skin shining from the sweat of his exertions, husked the coconuts. Bending over a fixed, erect metal knife, he deftly turned the green-yellow fruit around the sharp blade, cutting away the fibrous outside to reveal the hard brown nut. This discarded fibre, thrown onto an ever increasing pile, was collected to be made into coir rope. Another equally muscular man had his machete ready. With one well-aimed blow he cracked open each nut vertically to reveal the shining white interior. Using both hands he prised the hard shell apart, the wasted coconut water dripping off his fingers. A third man collected these opened nuts, carrying them into the drying sheds, placing them white side up onto rows of shelves. Here, charcoal slowly burned, creating a drying warmth which after a few days turned the white coconut flesh into a hard brown-yellow shrivelled shape, copra. This was and still is a commodity, sold by weight, used wherever coconut oil is needed.

The hard coconut shells were also sold to be used in many diverse ways: made into charcoal; attached to rubber trees to collect latex, or to gum trees to collect resin; used as a mould for prepared jaggery (sweet sap from the kittul palm which is boiled down until the dark brown consistency sets, tasting like heaven); fashioned into ladles for cooking, salad servers or toys. I had a turtle fashioned from the dark polished shell. His head and legs were hooked on under the shell, allowing movement. I kept him on a shelf above my bed, tapping him so he would appear to be swimming through the air, his little head moving from side to side.

These hard-working labourers were always happy when we came to visit, as it was a chance to pause in their back-breaking task. They stood erect, sweating and happy as my father asked questions about their work, bending with them to look at the white hard coconut; pressing, sniffing, tapping. I was proud of my handsome dad: relaxed; wearing his bush shirt, beige shorts and sandals; speaking Sinhala – not well, but enjoying practising, raising laughs with his mispronunciation. The air in the clearing was often heavy, and sweat trickled down our legs.

"Let's go to the rocks, Daddy. Please," I asked one day,

clambering back into the stuffy car. My father cautiously edged his way along the slippery sand until we could go no further. Parking under a shady tree, we scrambled up onto huge boulders, climbing, jumping, stepping over these smooth rocks until we found the most perfect spot to sit to catch late-afternoon breezes. The rocks were hot under my thighs. I moved around, pulling down the fabric of my shorts, trying to find a comfy spot. In front of us the river, bounded by dense green vegetation, was lazy, wide and brown, sliding into the nearby ocean. There was total silence, apart from the rustle of palm leaves, blown by a welcoming, gentle wind. Looking up I saw small wispy clouds patterning blue sky. My father quietly pointed to the left. A kingfisher was sitting, poised on an overhanging branch. There was a sudden flash of iridescent vivid turquoise as he dived for his catch. We watched a fisherman close to our vantage point balancing his catamaran, pulling in his net. We could see silver fish wriggling, twisting, caught up in the dark skeins, the man's broad smile wrinkling his weathered face. He was happy with his catch. Over by the far bank, other villagers were preparing their boats, about to head out to sea for their night's work. Their shouts drifted over on the air together with a smell of burning earth and acrid lantana, this ubiquitous bush with its bright orange and yellow flowers, which smothered scrub, managing to grow everywhere.

Jocelyn loved this place. I can see her in my mind's eye, leaning back, eyes closed, savouring the coolness on her skin. She is wearing a short-sleeved, well-fitting blouse, her hands wrapped around her knees, smiling. It's not often she is happy. She must be about thirty-four; such a pretty woman with her blonde curly hair and delicate complexion. She never sits in the sun. Like all women, born and bred in this land of contrasts, she fears the sun's rays. She dabs her ever-present hanky to her temples. Now I can smell 4711, where her cologne has permeated this useful cloth. My father sits, legs apart, elbows on knees, binoculars against his eyes, looking out towards the fishermen, curious, lost in this world of endless water, where life has remained unchanged for centuries.

Chapter 34

Moogie Doudney

"We have been invited to tea, down the coast towards Batticaloa, to a coconut estate run by a most fascinating woman called Moogie. She and George have been friends for many years and, like my mother, she was married here. She is a widow now, but still runs her estate. She can tell a good story; I think you will find her interesting. Moogie's son is a planter and has two grandsons at school with you, Richard and Ken Doudney." I knew the boys, both dark haired, handsome, sporty, one older, one younger than me. "Yes, I know them. Will they be there?" I asked, nervously. Perhaps my father felt I needed some company, but I was happy on my own. "I don't think so, but let's go and see."

So we piled into the small car, over the bridge, back onto the narrow road, and drove south, catching glimpses of the ocean through the trees. The sensation of hot air blowing through the open window onto my face, through my hair, was liberating. "Daddy, please turn up the music." Jocelyn was always quietly nervous, sitting in the front. I must have been a pain for her. My father and I were very alike and I enjoyed playing on that togetherness, probably making her feel uncomfortable. In those days, feelings weren't discussed. I was constantly ticked off for bad table manners, speaking too quickly, being told to listen to the 'grown-ups'. My father often did things I wasn't allowed to do. "Daddy, how come you are allowed to do that, and I'm not?" I would ask. "It's because I am grown up," was his standard reply. I didn't think much about his answer but I was not allowed to argue or answer back.

Row after row of palms, planted in straight lines, led away from either side of the road. "You see those on the right? The leaves are yellowing, they need fertiliser." Then, a little later, "Now those trees are healthy. Look over there, Judy. Their leaves are green, shiny." I looked, noticing the bunches of green nuts hanging together, bunched under the leaves at the top of the trunks. "That estate will have a good crop this year," Father said. Finally, he slowed down, turning into an entrance on the left where the sign read Mylanbavelly Estate. *What a romantic name*, I thought to myself. Looking at the palms growing on either side of the bumpy track, I assessed Moogie's chances of a good crop. They looked very healthy.

Moogie O'Dowd was born in Batticaloa in the eastern province of Ceylon. She had met Raymond, one of eight children, who had been born in Newcastle, arriving in Ceylon via America in 1896. They married two years later and bought Mylanbavelly coconut estate. My memories of this unusual, charismatic and tough lady are interwoven with many extraordinary stories she told us.

We had tea on her veranda, sitting on dark-wood Dutch furniture, being cooled by sea breezes and an ancient fan standing on a side table. Moogie must have been at least in her mid-seventies and energetic, full of talk. "Look at this, Judy," she said, showing me a beautiful, iridescent scarab beetle which had been crawling peacefully across the floor. Moogie picked it up. "The Egyptians worshipped these beetles; they were a sign of prosperity. They wore them as amulets." I gazed in wonder at this beautiful insect, in awe of this fascinating woman.

"Come outside with me." She walked down the steps over to a tall tree with pointed shiny leaves, full of yellow fruit. "Do you know what this is? It's a nutmeg tree. Look." Moogie stretched up, plucking off a fruit, breaking apart the yellow skin. Inside was a feathery red plastic, covering a brown nut. "This is mace." She peeled off the red. "Its flavour is similar to that of nutmeg, but softer. This is nutmeg," she said, taking the brown nut. "It's good for the digestion. You probably have it on the top of rice pudding, but if you take too much it can be hallucinogenic." She looked at me with her bright eyes. "You know, give you strange dreams!" I was fascinated. I had never heard that word before or met a woman like her.

Moogie told us a story which I have never forgotten.

"I was staying on a tea estate which my son Arthur was looking after for a while, while the PD, periya Dorai, tamil name for big master, estate manager, was on home leave. Arthur was due holiday so I went to keep an eye on things while he and his wife and the boys went on holiday. Before he left Arthur made sure I knew the ropes but he didn't know where the bedside plug for the light was. I told him not to fuss as I always slept with a torch under my pillow.

"I went to bed as usual but was woken by an unusual feeling. There, opposite me, was a woman standing by the door. I could clearly see her face. 'What are you doing sleeping here? Who are you?' she asked. I replied that I was looking after things for my son, who was on holiday. 'The bed is in the wrong place. It should be over there.' She pointed to the opposite corner of the room. 'What are you doing here?' she repeated. I wasn't frightened but extremely curious as to who this person could be. She just stood there. I said, 'I have a torch under my pillow. I want to see who you are.' I grabbed my torch, turned it on and she had gone. Well, I went back to sleep.

"The next morning I searched over by the corner where the strange woman had pointed and, sure enough, found a plug for the light. It was concealed behind a heavy chest. When Arthur and family returned after a week or so, I told him the story. 'Would you recognise this woman?' he asked. 'Oh yes, I saw her face clearly,' I said.

"A few days later, for some reason we were looking through a couple of photo albums on the bookcase. One was full of family pictures. Suddenly, over Arthur's shoulder, I saw a snapshot of my late-night visitor. 'Look, there is that woman, Arthur. Do you remember, I told you she gave me a bad time!' Arthur looked at me with a strange expression on his face. 'That is Sheila, the wife of Henry, the PD who is on leave at the moment.' We were stunned. I looked more closely, turned the page and found more photos of my ghostly visitor.

"I have thought about it quite a lot and can only suppose that she was having a bad dream about her home and did some time travel. Imagine when she found me in her house!"

I loved stories like this and Moogie always rose to the

occasion: "I have to tell you something else. I was keeping an eye on Passekudah for dear George. He and I were such good friends. He had to go to Colombo; he was not at all well. Late one night I heard a loud call for help. I put on my shoes, grabbed my torch and went outside. It was dark, silent, no moon. I shone my torch around, called out and walked around the perimeter of the bungalow. Towards the back I met the night-watchman. 'Lady, what are you doing outside?' he said. 'I heard someone calling for help but I can't find anyone,' I replied. 'I heard that call as well,' he said. For a while we walked around together. We looked in the kitchen, the store, but found no one. I went to bed. Next day we received a telegram from Colombo telling us George had died during the night. It was very specific as it said he had died at 2.30am. That was the time the watchman and I heard his call. Dear George, I miss him very much."

Chapter 35

Swimming Races

Eva and I were growing up. During our holidays we met at the pool. We played for hours – tag, swimming lengths against each other, throwing coins into the water to collect from the bottom and practising our diving from the coir-covered springboard. We ordered Vimto and cashew nuts from the bar boy, feeling very adult, signing the bar chits. Then we lay in the striped saggy deckchairs, holding the ice-cold bottles against our arms, while the red drink stained our mouths. Crows cawed and flapped overhead, queuing on the top of the shade roof, waiting for their chance to grab a nut when we had become too engrossed in our chat to shoo them away.

There was to be a swimming meet on a Saturday afternoon. The air was electric. We had signed up for the under-eights 33⅓ -yard freestyle sprint. Silver cups were cordoned off, standing on a table covered with a white cloth, along with the rest of the prizes. Our fathers looked very important dressed in their office clothes, white short-sleeved shirts but with long, pressed cream trousers for this important day. Conferring together, they gathered at the start and finish lines with their stopwatches and clipboards. Eva and I waited with our age group at the deep end, hearts pounding, mouths dry. Called to the start, we stood as Harry had taught us – toes just over the black non-slip edge, gripping hard, knees apart and bent, back straight, arms back, eyes forward. The gun sounded and we were off. Stretching through the air, splashing into the water, then kick, kick, kicking our legs as hard as we could, pulling our arms through, scooping the water, fingers together like a cup, one breath to four strokes, not slowing down at the end, racing until our fingers touched the wall. "Come on, Judy Ann. You can do it!" I could hear Harry's words in my head as I pounded down the lane, the roar of the onlookers faint in my ears.

To my surprise I came first, just beating Eva. She excelled at breaststroke, winning her race. Later, dressed in a cotton swimming robe, I was presented with a small silver cup. Everyone clapped, especially as it appeared to be a record time, meaning my name would go up in gold letters on the wooden board in the clubhouse. I felt very embarrassed and proud.

After the prize-giving we sat with our parents in the warm dusk, terrace lights attracting evening insects, eating hot, salty homemade chips with spicy tomato ketchup. Our wet hair dripped down our backs. We were happy after all the tensions.

Chapter 36

Toddy Tappers

Some weekends were spent south at Bentota, en route to Galle. Ahh, Bentota. How that name still brings joyous images to mind. A single-track railway line wound down the coast, close to the road. At times the road crossed the tracks – bump, bump – with no guard rails or warning lights as the noisy trains were infrequent. Startling images of brilliant blue sea would appear in front, only to be hidden again by dense trees, houses or small villages. This narrow road, the main artery to the south, was always full of traffic: overloaded buses belching out black fumes, bicycles, bullock carts, pedestrians and dogs; skinny, mangy – accidents waiting to happen.

We had started this particular journey early on a Saturday morning. Even at this hour it was slow going out through the congested suburbs, past the turning to Dehiwala Zoo, Panadura, the place for wooden items, which were displayed along the roadside, the smell of freshly cut timber blowing in through the window. My excitement mounted driving over the Kalu Ganga bridge, seeing sand banks to the right, smelling the sea in the distance before turning towards Kalutara, famous for its basket weaving.

My father pointed upwards: "Look, the toddy tappers

are at work." Rope walkways had been strung from palm to palm just under the crown of the trees, linking them all together. Pa slowed down, stopped on the edge of the road. "Look carefully, Judy. We don't often see them on this journey. The tappers have to finish their work before it gets too warm. Look at that man. See his knife? He is cutting the end of the coconut flower bud. He will tie rope around the cut, put a pot underneath to collect the sap. Tomorrow he will come to empty the liquid." It looked dangerous work. Dressed only in a loincloth, the tapper now carefully walked along the rope to the next palm tree. Here he emptied the sap into a larger pot attached to his waist by rope which looped over his shoulder. Calling to his assistant waiting below, he gently lowered the pot, hand over hand, to the ground. His companion poured the contents into a large container, then shouted for the empty pot to be pulled up.

We watched a little longer. The tapper was like an acrobat, balancing on his precarious, swaying line, grasping the rope above him as he walked from tree to tree. When he had finished his round, he slipped a circle of rope around his ankles, gripped the palm trunk with his bare soles, arms and hands and slid down. It looked effortless.

"Toddy is fermented coconut sap, just a few days old, a little like beer. Arrack is distilled from toddy. It's rather like whisky, quite a strong taste. The local men drink toddy; they get pretty drunk and start fighting." "Don't they ever fall off?" I asked. "Oh yes, it's a dangerous job, especially if they have been drinking the night before. The trees and job are usually handed down from father to son."

The tapper had reached the ground safely. Well muscled, slim and agile, he joked with his companion as he unwrapped his sarong, letting it fall loose around his legs. Putting on his shirt, the two of them lifted the full toddy container to the edge of the road. "They wait for the bullock cart to come with the cask, then it's taken to the distillery. They are dotted all down the coast." My father seemed to know everything.

We drove on past Beruwala Harbour, where fishing boats clustered together, resting from their pre-dawn journeys.

"Are we nearly there, Daddy?" I was a poor traveller, always feeling sick, impatient in the back of the car. "Start counting the milestones. Not far to go now," he reassured me.

Bentota Ganga, a wide, lazy river, flowed out to sea, leaving behind a narrow isthmus on its south, seaward side. An ugly brown metal bridge, its middle span supported by a large lump of rock in the middle of the river, was shared by trains and cars. Bentota Rest House, its thatched palm roof level with the top of the coconut palms bordering the sea, was built on rock on the south side of the bridge. Stunning sea views, spicy fish curry, fresh lime sodas and beers after a refreshing swim had attracted travellers to this spot for years. From the rest house the finger of land stretched half a mile northwards, parallel with the coast – sea on one side, palm trees and river on the other. A small rocky island stood at the tip, complete with a Buddhist temple where a hermit monk lived. Southwards from the tip, past the rest house to the next rocky headland, was the stunning beach of Bentota Bay. Miles of clean golden sand.

This magnificent piece of land was the perfect weekend hideaway. Several people had built discreet thatched bungalows under the palms on the isthmus between the rest house and temple island. To reach these retreats, we had to turn off the main road close to the thirty-seventh milestone and bump along a rutted track until we could see the river through the trees.

We parked the old Morris under the palms in a garden, close to a small jetty. The sarong-clad house owner came over, salaamed and welcomed us. "I call boat," he smiled, helping us with our luggage. All of us were happy to have arrived safely as the Colombo to Galle road was notorious for accidents. Standing waiting in the shade under the rustling palms, ocean smell strong in the air, watching the small motor boat power its way across the river, my excitement knew no bounds.

Clambering aboard, our careful boatman stowed our bags before he opened up the engine, steering us across the river to… heaven. With the river on one side and sea with an endless two-mile beach on the other, the narrow spit of Bentota was covered with palms. Our friends had a simple palm-thatched house built in typical style with a veranda running around the outside. A bucket of fresh well water stood beside the entrance steps. "Feet must be rinsed before you come inside."

Bathing costume covered with a sarong was the dress code, followed by a late breakfast after we all had walked the length of the beach, swum and showered. Lif and Mark's daughter, Gillian, now four years old, was just the right age for me to look after. At low tide the river bank was exposed, allowing a flat space for safe swimming and jumping off the jetty. I stood up to my waist in the water, feet balancing on the soft river mud, catching Gillian as she jumped into the river, laughing with joy, splashing and kicking towards me, wanting to do it over and over again. The older members of the weekend party water-skied, swam and drank beer, relaxing under the palms in rattan chairs, telling stories, waiting for the cook to produce a gargantuan curry lunch.

In the mid-fifties there were few buildings on this spit. At night after dinner the generator was turned off and silence reigned. All we could hear were waves gently breaking, palms rustling under the breeze. Stars weighed down, filling an immense sky.

Chapter 37

Another Boarding School

The time approached for some of us to be sent to boarding school in England. I was now ten years old. "I never saw my parents from one year to the next," said my father. He had been a boarder at Lancing College, up on the hill close to Brighton, Sussex. His words filled me with dread; I couldn't bear the thought of being so far away. "Where shall I spend my holidays, Daddy? I don't want to go back to England. It's cold and dark. I want to stay here, with you."

At the Hill School, 'home' was referred to constantly. This was England, where grandparents, aunts and uncles lived, not our homes with our parents in Ceylon. Children would miss a term of school, because they were 'on home leave'. Planters and office workers were allowed four to six months' home leave every three years. This allowed time for a sea passage back and forth, time to renew family and friendship bonds, to breathe the air, to take in theatre, culture, eat apples, cheeses, to buy good-quality shoes, to have respite from the monotonous heat. For my parents and those of my friends, 'home' became a place in the mind, a refuge of happy memories; a place which was safe, secure, faraway, over the sea, where their parents lived, where everything worked properly, to where most colonials longed to return.

Growing up with 'home' being referred to almost as a sanctuary, there must have been an unspoken acceptance amongst us that we all would be sent there for schooling, sooner or later. Those with older siblings who had already gone home to school were more used to the notion than I was, ostensibly an only child. The reality that I was being sent away again to school, 6,000 miles away, was shocking indeed.

There was an international school in Colombo which took youngsters up to O level stage. Possibly as a result of the fears aroused in me when first sent to school in Colombo, after Nicola was left behind in England, or following advice from our headmaster at the Hill School, Mr Spurrier, a decision had been made. I never thought to ask why. In the fifties children were not consulted about major decisions which seriously affected their lives. We were discouraged from answering back. "I never saw my family," was all my father would say. Subject closed. It appeared that what had happened to my father, his siblings and my stepmother and her sister Gill, was going to happen to me. It was all extremely unsettling.

"We have discussed this with Aunty Joan and Uncle Bill. Joan is looking forward to being your guardian while we are here in Ceylon. We shall all sail back to England together for our home leave so we are there for the start of your new school term in September."

I learned my fate. September was six months away. I felt sick with nerves, quite unable to imagine how life would be. I scarcely knew my aunt and my uncle. I remembered a thin, tall, forbidding-looking man who had quite terrified me on the one occasion I had met him.

I had a small plastic water-filled dome with a model of the Houses of Parliament inside. When I shook it, snow appeared and covered the building, slowly subsiding when I put it down.

Snow, I thought, *I have never seen that.*

At Christmas our families sent cards decorated with snow-encrusted holly, often with a red-breasted robin nearby, or pictures of pink-cheeked children, laughing, sledging, or sometimes churches with pointed spires standing in snowy graveyards, with graceful evergreen trees, their branches weighed down with snow. They conjured up beautiful images, the antithesis of our Christmas days spent on the beach, shading ourselves under palm fronds, out of the burning sun.

Perhaps that will be exciting, I mused, having little conception of those freezing cold, long, dark evenings.

Father's sister Joan lived in the village of Alresford, in Hampshire. For many years Bill had been a tea taster in Calcutta. There are pictures of the family with Joan and Bill, soon after they married, all together up country at the house near Hakgala. They lived in India many years before returning 'home'.

Now he worked for a tea-broking firm, commuting to the London office. I scarcely knew them or their two children, Mark and Sara. I was becomingly increasingly anxious, wondering where I would sleep, what I may have to wear, whether I would be able to swim, which at that time was my biggest passion.

"Do you know what school you are going to, Eva?"

I asked the next time I saw her. Like me she was feeling nervous, unsure about a huge lifestyle change. "Not yet," she replied. "I have to take some exams and then I have to pass them." She screwed up her normally cheerful face. "But Mummy and Daddy have some good friends who will look after me during the holidays." Her parents had escaped from Czechoslovakia after the war. Still stateless, they were waiting for papers to allow them to live in America. "I hope we are somewhere close to each other. I hope we can ride horses and see the snow!"

My parents had chosen a school in West Sussex. I am sure parents at that time, when they met up with their friends, discussed their options and the costs, but most importantly, which school. It appeared that a few girls I already knew were being sent to this particular place. Certainly my Dutch girlfriend Patty was; she was in my class at the Hill School. Patty had two younger brothers. They took after their father, and all were sports mad; a close, happy, together family. One year her father had presented the prizes at our sports day, so he remained in my mind as a very important person. *If Patty is going as well, it may not be so bad*, I thought.

All my belongings had to be packed away. Nothing could be left in cupboards or drawers. Not only did leather shoes become covered with green mould – as did any black dress or trousers, it was so humid – but cockroaches and other insects always chewed their way through the most precious objects.

I had a large box on which I wrote, in big black letters: LOOK IN HERE OFTEN. I filled it with my precious collection of white china horses, small Chinese figures and my ballet dancer collection. Every year for my birthday I was given one of these small, delicate figurines. My favourite was dressed in a blue tutu, balancing on points. Every day I rearranged my dancers. Voraciously I had read all the Lorna Hill and Noel Streatfeild ballet books, requesting the latest story for my birthdays. Oh, how I had dreamed! I longed to be a dancer. Endlessly I drew ballet shoes on any spare piece of paper, always with the foot in the point position, satin ribbon straps wound around the lower leg. When the house was empty I put on the vinyl recording of *La Boutique fantasque* and turned up the volume, spinning across the room, gliding and pirouetting, my bare feet sliding on the red polished tiles. Waltzing down the steps onto the open top of the porch, where the cement was rough and burning underfoot, the brightness and heat of midday warming my soul, I flung my arms wide into the sky, dreaming, circling, moving in time with the music.

Chapter 38

Going Back 'Home'

My trunk, now a well-battered dirty brown, had arrived home the last time from the Hill School, my uniform ousted, unneeded. I asked to be taken to the swimming club. The driver dropped me off at the entrance. I quickly changed, ran and dived into the comforting water. Starting my lengths, up and down, up and down, I stared at the blue tiles and black lines on the bottom of the pool as the water surged past me, anxious feelings filling my entire body – *I don't want to go, I'm not going, I don't want to leave home...* Somehow the negative words fitted in with the rhythm of my arms. But slowly the strong movement calmed me. My breathing became more laboured as I swam on and on and my mind emptied. My focus was kicking my legs evenly, swinging my arms while allowing my thumb to brush against my hip, touching the tiled wall at each end, flipping around and starting the next length. I loved the sensation of gliding through the water, safe from the world, tucked inside my own place; secure, free.

Often, at evening time in Colombo, we had walked along the breakwater close to the harbour, looking at all the ships, noting where they were registered, watching crew members leaning over the rails and smoking, relaxing like us. Valparaiso, Hamburg, Rotterdam – the names painted in large letters on their rusty prows evoked foreign lands, exciting travel.

Now it was our turn. All our suitcases and packages were piled alongside us in the launch which cut through the water, taking us once more to the Bibby Liner, for the start of our journey back home.

This time the waves were high and the boat rolled from side to side as I stood at the ship's bow watching the dolphins swim alongside in perfect unison, diving in and out of the wake. Every day, for hours, I watched these beautiful creatures who were accompanying us through the Indian Ocean.

First stop was Aden, nestling beneath a circle of dry, barren rocky mountains, squat buildings on the foreshore. From there we entered the Red Sea, sailing north-west to reach Port Sudan.

"Come on, Judy. Let's go in the glass-bottomed boat. The captain tells me the coral here is superb." My father was excited – he was on holiday: no more hot, stuffy office or responsibility for a while. He had six months' home leave and the first thing he would do once he was home was to visit Nicola.

We walked down the sloping gangplank together. The glare pricked my eyes. Dust was in the air as the Sudanese port workers, their skin dark and shiny in the heat, were placing nets around large bags strapped onto crates, attaching them onto the enormous hook of the crane. Swinging high into the air, gently turning, swaying from side to side, the bundles were lowered into our ship's hold. "What's in there, Daddy? What are they loading?"

"That load is sugar. Sudan is a big exporter. This cargo is coming all the way to England with us." I felt comfortable with my father; he always answered my questions and seemed to know everything.

Chapter 39

Coral Reefs

The glass-bottomed boat wobbled as we climbed aboard, carefully sitting on a hard wooden bench, a dirty cotton dhury tied to four supports affording us shade. Skilfully, the boatman manoeuvred his small boat into the deep harbour. I was mesmerised, my eyes glued to the glass floor. Bright, clear water swirled below. I could see fish gliding past. We sped towards the rocks beyond the harbour's entrance where our guide slowed down.

"Look, look," he smiled, pointing, his perfect teeth white in his dark face, his hair ragged.

Suddenly, bank after bank of the most perfectly formed branches of coral appeared below us. Red, pink, white tipped with blue, orange… Home to myriads of brightly coloured fish – striped, spotted, black, yellow – darting in and out of the branches. We floated quietly as eels slid along the sand and a turtle drifted past. Large football fish with pointed top fins swam along, shoals of tiny silver fish moved as one, back and forth.

Later that day my father found me with a book, lying on my bunk. "Come up on deck, there is something you must see." We leaned against the wooden rails side by side, the evening breeze cool on our faces, watching row after row of white-robed men, all facing the same direction, each one wearing a bright red tasselled fez. "Allahu Akbar… God is Great," called the mullah from the top of the mosque. With one smooth movement these men knelt down on their prayer mats, prostrating themselves, touching their heads to the ground.

"What are they doing, Daddy?" I asked. "These are the port workers we saw earlier. They have finished their work for the day. It's sunset and prayer time now. You heard the mullah call. They are all facing towards Mecca, in Saudi Arabia." He pointed towards the south.

I loved my father and these special moments we had together. I tried not to think of what was ahead for me. Finally, I had become used to boarding school, having already spent four years in Nuwara Eliya, but this time I was being left alone – my beloved father would be far away. My heart lurched; the sick feeling in my belly appeared. I pushed dark thoughts away.

Continuing our journey up the Red Sea, we sailed through to the Lakes, where we waited our turn to pass through the Suez Canal. The banks were so narrow it seemed the boat was being squeezed tight, that we might scrape the sides. Standing at the rails with the road running along at eye level, I became absorbed watching robed men sitting on their straw-laden carts, pulled by donkeys. Groups of scrawny children playing on the bank waved and shouted at us; men on bicycles, a few cars, all travelling past, all raising dust as they went about their day's work. I was so close to these Egyptian country people and we were moving so gently, so slowly, it was peaceful, dreamlike, and for those few moments I felt I was part of their life.

At Port Said, while our boat was provisioned, small boys swam alongside, splashing to catch our attention, shouting, "Coin, coin!" We threw shining pennies into the air. They watched, then dived, catching the coins as they floated down through the clear water, bobbing up, holding up their hands, laughing, vying for the best place. Small boats arrived alongside, rowed by turbaned men, their decks piled high with wares of leather pouffes, stuffed camels, dates, small hookahs, inlaid boxes. Furious bartering took place over the side of the boat, the passengers all shouting, straining over the rail high above the sea, the men below looking up, balancing precariously in their small boats. My father joined in. Finally, he agreed a price. The boatman, well practised, deftly threw a rope up for us to catch. "Hold on," said my father. He pulled on the rope – up and up. Over the rail came a flattened leather pouffe, together with a battered purse into which he put the agreed money and untied our purchase. Taking aim he dropped the rope over the side. I sniffed at the leather, felt the worked pattern with my fingers. The gold figures were stylised. "Next time you come home I shall have filled this and it will be yours to sit on when you read my papers!"

Day by day, England was getting closer; the Bay of Biscay had to be crossed. It was always this rough stretch of water, together with its overcast skies, when we all put on warm clothes and retired to our cabins. The heaving and swaying was the first realisation that we were in the northern hemisphere. The sea was grey, echoed by the sky, and the wind blew slanting sheets of rain which hit the deck, dripping from the rails. Few passengers filled the dining room. The change of atmosphere was palpable. Although my parents were looking forward to their holiday, I was facing the unknown. Huddling in my bunk, covered with heavy blankets, my belly queasy, I was too miserable to read.

Chapter 40

Nicola

Our first visit was to see Nicola in Haywards Heath. She had grown up. She was taller and broader, like a stranger. I sensed she scarcely knew who I was.

"Hello, Nico!" I felt shy with my sister, who spoke jerkily, her voice deep, her manner strange. "Hello, Judy." She wrapped her arms around me, squeezing me tight, lifting me off the ground. She felt soft, warm. She held me hard, tight; my breath was trapped in my chest. She was strong. I felt embarrassed, uncomfortable. We didn't touch as a family. Nicola lifted me higher, putting her face close to mine, then letting me go she wandered off, muttering to herself. I didn't know what to do, what to say to her. My father caught her; held her, hugged her. How painful it must have been for him; how he must have longed to see her, been wracked with guilt. He never spoke about his feelings. Nicola must have suffered as well during these years, thousands of miles apart from her family. She didn't have the vocabulary to describe her feelings; her language was extremely limited.

But Mrs Farrer Brown had nurtured and cared for Nicola, along with eight other young children who had some sort of disability, all of whom lived in her spacious house. Over the last four years she had been sending regular progress reports to my father. *When Nicola is thirteen, she will be too old to stay with me. I am trying to arrange a place for her at The Royal Earlswood Institution, near Redhill. I think this might be the best place for her to live when she leaves me. I shall be very sad. How long will you be here this time? Perhaps we can organise a visit for you and your wife? That may help the selection process.*

All these years later I realise the terrible decisions my father was forced to make for his daughters. After the end of this holiday, he was only allowed home leave every three years. He would have to leave me at boarding school, finalise moving Nicola to another home, and then sail back to Colombo with Jocelyn.

My father's mother, whom I called Granny Burns, sometimes Granny B if I felt brave, was now living in Reigate in a pretty three-bedroom house in a cul-de-sac, opposite a spinney. She had aged into quite a formidable character, always wearing a black or navy long-sleeved dress, covered in a small flowery pattern, softened with a lace ruffle around the neck. We based ourselves with Granny, revelling in the long, light summer evenings. In the tropics the sun set quickly at the same time each day, bringing mosquitoes, fireflies and croaking frog sounds from the irrigation department on the opposite side of the road into the warm darkness. Here I was able to play outside in Granny's garden until late, help with her vegetables, look at her roses and lavender, breathe in their perfume. These English flowers, delicate and stylish, were so different to the orchids, brightly coloured gerbera daisies and red quisqualis creeper in our tropical garden.

The Munday brothers, who lived next door, befriended me. I fell madly in love with Paul, who played the clarinet, and when it was bedtime, if he was practising, I would listen to the liquid notes drifting in through my window.

Granny's milkman had a horse which pulled the milk float. Each day after their round, Granny quickly took her bucket and shovel to collect any horse droppings she might find on the road. She placed this around her roses. Then she put the two milk bottles into a brown crock, which stood in water to keep it cool. The larder faced north and had a small open window covered with thick metal gauze. This allowed in cool air as there was no fridge.

I was always up early and loved to take Granny her early morning tea. "I have it very weak please, Judy. Only a few leaves!" Solemnly I measured the long dried leaves into the pot, covered them with boiling water, put on the cosy and placed the pot on her little tray, together with a cup, saucer and milk jug. Carefully I carried this upstairs, knocking on her door. "Come in," she'd call. I would find her expectantly lying up against her pillows. "Good morning, Granny," I'd say, placing the tea beside her bed. There was a strong urine smell as she had a potty under her bedside table. I drew her curtains and peeped at her calendar. The picture turned pink if the weather was set fair and blue if it was going to rain.

Chapter 41

Sainsbury's

My father revelled in being back home, doing everything to excess; all those things he couldn't do in Ceylon.

"Let's go into town and buy some cheese and coffee." He bundled me into the car and we drove down the hill, past the common and the station, through the tunnel to Reigate centre, parking outside Sainsbury's. The shop's name, written on black, was above the door. Long marble counters displayed meats, cheeses, bread. Queues formed for each section and there was a quiet hum of voices. Everything was clean, orderly, the smell of fresh bread in the air.

Pa sniffed the various coffee beans and made his choice. Then it was ground, the heady aroma filling our nostrils, and poured into a brown paper package and sealed by the assistant. Next we queued for cheese, which he loved; the stronger and smellier the better. He'd always give me a small piece to try, so I learned early to appreciate different flavours. Next stop was the hardware shop. Pa was going to put up a shelf for his mother and needed screws. He was very practical and loved fixing things around the house.

Back to Granny's, where by now, I was feeling a bit more at home, although the thought of this new school was ever present. I had been given a table in a corner of the sitting room where I had my colours and books. Every afternoon I listened to Children's Hour on the radio, while colouring intricate patterns. Granny had a delicately painted china house on her mantelpiece. The top lifted off and a candle would throw light out of the tiny windows.

A new trunk arrived. Again it was brown. Pa stencilled my initials on the side, this time in black paint. He blurred them a little, the S on one side. For years after this, every time I saw these letters I remembered my father, bending over, using a small paintbrush, carefully painting in my initials. For him, it must have been an act of love. For me, one of banishment.

Inside the top of the trunk was a cream-coloured cloth tray which could be lifted out using small handles at the sides. It smelt fresh, unused. This was for light objects, such as vests and pants, collars and my weekend mufti dresses. Standing in my bedroom against the wall, this benign object filled me with fear of the unknown.

A list of clothes and items needed for the term had been sent from school:

1 brown Harris Tweed overcoat with matching beret
2 brown Harris Tweed skirts, with front pleat
2 emerald-green woollen twinsets
4 collars
1 brown cloak
1 pair brown indoor shoes
1 pair outdoor shoes
1 pair galoshes
1 pair games shoes

2 pairs brown games skirts
3 aertex shirts

And so the list went on until it reached:

3 pairs brown overpants
6 pairs cotton liners

We had to wear over and underpants, every day. If we were caught without the brown pants, we were in serious trouble. Each week they were sent to the bag wash, along with our sweaters. None of us knew what this bag wash meant, we just stuffed them into a big cotton bag, making rude jokes.

We wore our collars, which had a bib down the back and front, held together by elastic, under our sweaters.

The summer clothing list had extras:

3 cotton dresses
1 bottle-green tweed suit (a different green to our sweaters,
this was for Sundays)
1 green hat
1 silk shantung dress
1 felt hat

Our felties always had to be worn in the sun. We pulled them out of shape and wrote on them. Some appeared to be partly eaten, but undeterred, our headmistress, Mrs Brown, or Ma B always lectured us on the strength of the sun. I wish I had taken her seriously all those years ago.

My father must have blanched when he realised the

cost of this uniform. The silk dresses were printed and very pretty. I hardly remember wearing mine as it never seemed to be hot enough. All my uniform was new. Kinch & Lack, the official school outfitters, or Pinch and Slack, as they became known amongst us, must have made a killing. There certainly were no second-hand clothes shops in 1955.

Chapter 42

The Day Arrives

Finally, the September day arrived.

I put on my new uniform: white vest and pants complete with the brown overpants. Already I was feeling hot. Next, the cream collar. I stretched the elastic down around my waist. Now the emerald-green woollen pullover. I hated the sensation of heaving a woollen sweater over my face, pushing my arms through the narrow sleeves. Pulling the collar out around the neck, I looked in the mirror. What a horrible, strong colour. The wool pricked against my skin. I felt anxious, very unhappy. It was too warm to put on the matching cardigan. My brown Harris Tweed skirt was heavy, long. It reached mid-calf, with a double flat pleat down the front to allow enough movement for walking. I zipped it up and did up the button at the side. It felt cumbersome, and scratched against my legs. There was a small pocket on the right for a handkerchief. I wore knee-length light-brown socks and my outdoor lace-up brown shoes. My overcoat and beret sat on the bed. The coat, standard length, came below my skirt, nearly to my ankles.

The reflection in the mirror threw back a picture of a well-built eleven-year-old girl; shoulder-length dark hair cut in a bob, with a sallow complexion. My Ceylon tan which always brought out my freckles had already faded in the English climate, and like most young brought up in the tropics, our skin never had the peaches-and-cream English look. I looked at myself, feeling stupid in all the heavy clothes, wondering what on earth was ahead of me. I looked scared, defensive. I felt sick, uncomfortable.

Everything was put in the car. I gave my Granny a hug. I am sure she knew what I was going through, and how my father must be feeling. She had sent all her children to boarding school, so she understood heartbreak. She stood at the top steps of her front garden where the beds were bright with asters and Michaelmas daisies, her neat rockery leading down to the pavement. She appeared so solid, dressed in black, waving goodbye as we moved away, down the hill.

The school was perched in a hollow below the South Downs. From Midhurst the road was narrow and twisty, in some parts single track, where the banks stretched up high on either side, blocking out the light. Slowly negotiating the bends, squeezed into our Morris Minor, my trunk on the roof, we made our way up this lane until the view exploded to our left. We could see all the way towards the sea. We reached the lodge house at the entrance to the school, crossed the cattle grid – rattle, rattle, rattle – and down the narrow track, fields on either side, fenced with barbed wire. We passed the hangar from where the Duchess of Bedford, an earlier owner, had made her last, fateful flight, and continued down towards the school buildings. Then round the bend between banks of rhododendron bushes, still driving downwards to the right, and finally, turning to the left we saw rows of larger and smarter cars than ours, parked outside an imposing white and black timbered house.

We had arrived. My heart lurched. There was silence in the car as Pa turned off the ignition. I knew that very soon, when my trunk was inside that hateful front door, my parents would return to their car, drive away and in a few days sail back to Colombo, the car going with them as well.

I was going to be totally alone.

Chapter 43

Apple

Arranging my photograph frame on my bedside locker, I looked out of the large, black-framed windows of Robins dormitory. The gardens on this side of the house, bounded by rhododendron bushes, sloped away towards fields, the South Downs in the distance, with plenty of sky above. Closer by stood tall trees, evergreen with spreading branches, statuesque against a smooth green lawn. Two of these trees had a wide white line painted on their trunks, halfway up. "We can climb those trees, the ones with the white line. We aren't allowed any higher." My pilot knew everything about the school and was appointed to help me during my first few weeks. I was her aeroplane. Her name was Patty du Pon. She had been at school with me in Ceylon and our families were friends, but she had already been at this school for a term. My parents had chosen this place as many children from Ceylon were boarding here, the supposition being that we would keep each other company or that the school would be 'alright'. As I said earlier, there had been no discussion. I appeared to be a pawn in this game of life, being pushed around, told to behave, be a good girl, not to cry when my parents abandoned me in this dark valley in Sussex.

Our dormitory had ten beds – five against the window,

five against the back wall, and a built-in cupboard for our hanging clothes. At the far end, next to a closed fireplace, a chest of drawers held our clothes. This was a country house, converted into a school after the war. The floors were parquet; it was always cold. Matron's room was down the corridor. Miss Appleford, or Apple as everyone called her, took great care of us. She was curvaceous and white-haired, even though she wasn't old, and we all came to love her. She was strict. No noise after lights out. I was often in trouble for talking. I still hadn't learned to keep my mouth shut and spent quite a few dark evenings standing at the bottom of the great staircase outside the headmistress's study in my dressing gown and slippers – the penalty for being caught out.

I still have my blue and green tartan blanket which was an essential item on our school list. It was for extra warmth at night. My name tape, still attached, reads J.J.SHATTOCK in blue. Then another tape, in red: 94. It was my school number. I felt like a prisoner. I don't know who had the job to sew these tapes on my uniform, Jocelyn probably, but the separate number must have been a nuisance for her as it is so tiny, an afterthought perhaps. I was never actually called 94 and don't know why we all had a number, but it had to be put on every possession. Now the rug has moth holes and has faded badly from being left in the sun on the top lawn for three months by my daughters, who loved to lie on it when sunbathing. But I put it over my bedclothes on the top of my green paisley feather-filled counterpane every night for warmth.

I hated those cold days and nights. Dressed in our green twinsets, collars, vests, two pairs of knickers, long brown socks with garters, thick brown Harris Tweed skirts and brown shoes, we must all have looked a funny sight. Certainly we were bundled up, made to walk in crocodile wherever we went, certainly up to the hangar every day for gym or indoor games. It was always raining and how the wind blew as we walked up the uneven road past the music rooms, where notes of piano scales or a Chopin waltz floated into the air.

Our coats, outdoor shoes and sports kit were kept in a dark locker room, next to the toilets, opening off the Covered Way.

Everything seemed to happen in the Covered Way, with its cold, damp concrete floor and plastic moss-covered roof, which let in light and on which the endless rain made loud, rhythmic, tapping music. We simply looked upwards to check the weather. The notice board stood there, the kitchen faced it and classrooms opened off from it. Crates of small, silver-topped milk were put there at break time. We opened the milk bottle top, pressing firmly with a fingernail onto the foil, pushing in a short straw. It was rich, creamy and cold, the bottles dripping wet outside. Sometimes the milk was accompanied by bread and dripping, sometimes buns.

A light, airy room with wide, open views towards the Downs opened off the Covered Way, where we did basket weaving, sewing and music appreciation, activities suitable for 'nice young ladies'. Our sewing boxes, another necessary, labelled item, were stored in this room, along with library books and cane for weaving. Beyond the classrooms was the pottery shed, filled with a smell of damp clay. A potter's wheel stood in the centre on a raised dais. Once a week, dressed in overalls, we were let loose, squeezing, pressing, rolling, pounding the cold clay into small pots, plates or small figures, which we painted before they were fired hard enough to be taken home at the end of term.

Chapter 44

Mrs Brown and Miss Rogers

Our headmistress, Mrs Brown, Ma B to us, was a vicar's daughter and a vicar's widow. She and Miss Rogers, assistant head of school, Podge being her nickname, lived in the small lodge at the top of the drive. Ma B had permed white hair, a gentle face and an ample bosom, over which her hands appeared to be permanently folded. Podge, tall, lithe, of severe expression, ruled the school extremely firmly. Woe betide any girl who transgressed. It was a conduct mark immediately, or at the very, very worst, a stripe, straight out. This consisted of six conduct marks and six stripes meant you were expelled from school. A conduct mark was given out for not wearing brown knickers or for swearing, shouting, or even sneezing too loudly. One girl got into deep trouble for reading *Lady Chatterley's Lover* while walking around the games pitch, the incriminating book hidden beneath her brown cloak. That caused a serious scandal. I can remember that she was sporty and skinny with black curly hair and freckles, but not whether she was expelled. We couldn't wait to get our hands on 'the book'.

We were allowed to bring three reading books at the start of term, which we left in a pile outside Ma B's study. If she didn't approve of your choice, the book was returned at the end of term. Otherwise we found the book with HB scrawled in the front corner, and were free to read. What control. I bet those two had some fun going through our choices.

Jacky arrived at start of term with me. She had recently returned from Kenya, regaling us with stories of Mau Mau atrocities: "I had to sleep with a gun under my pillow." We stared at her aghast, not quite believing her story. Tall and slim, Jacky had long, narrow, elegant feet clad in shiny brown shoes, complete with strap and button. They curved inwards at the toe, giving her an awkward look.

Another girl, Jane, came from Woking. With her long dark plaits and pale face, she was shorter than Jacky and me, but we became firm friends, known as the 'three J's'.

School life settled into a routine of lessons, games, mealtimes and wearing of mufti on weekend evenings. I had a soft, brown corduroy dress with pretty trim. One day I found it slashed, ruined, hanging in the cupboard. *Who could have done that?* I wondered.

I loved my ballet classes. One day my ballet tunic was cut to shreds. Everyone was mystified. My Bible was scribbled in, pages cut – things became worse. Shoes were misplaced and I spent hours in the dank, smelly cloakroom searching for items which had gone missing. A girl in a class above me had been at the Hill School with me. She had spread malicious stories about me the term before I arrived. She was probably jealous of me, I realise now. I was unpopular from the start. My athletic prowess and cleverness in class did not help me.

Neither did the fact that I talked about Ceylon all the

time. I was miserable. I longed for the sun and warmth, my parents. These English girls were so strange.

It was a hard time. Finally my headmistress bundled me off to Harley Street to see a psychiatrist. So every Monday, Apple escorted me by train from Haslemere to Waterloo. My parents must have had plenty of extra additions to the school bill. The outcome was hazy. I had to do ink blob tests and recount my dreams, but worst of all, I missed my maths lessons and never managed to catch up.

Chapter 45

31 Broad Street

Aunty Joan, practical, steady and loving in a quiet way, had given me the use of her spare room during the holidays. This was very grand with a washbasin, mirror and light switch on a string inside a folding cupboard, all for my very own use. Sharing my aunt and uncle's home with my two cousins and later with Frank, Uncle Bill's nephew who had grown up in Rhodesia and was now at college in England, was never easy. I am sure my aunt had discussed all her plans at length with my parents and Bill. As usual, us children were just told what was to happen.

The spare room, situated on the landing between the lavatory and big family bathroom with its glorious view down the garden, was not the ideal place for me to be, probably because Joan and Bill wanted to keep it for their visitors. I was moved to another room, the steep stairs to which stood behind a door directly at the top of the main staircase. It was quite cut off from the rest of the house. On the small landing opposite the entrance of this room was a curtain covering a large space where our suitcases were stored. I never looked behind the curtain.

I could never sleep in that room. Something was wrong. It was extremely narrow with a high window overlooking the street, and enclosed and hot in the summer. I would be restless, calling out at night, frightened, worried with dreams. I can't remember whether anyone heard me crying but finally, I was moved again, to share my girl cousin's bedroom. I am sure she wasn't too happy with this arrangement.

Soon Maggie arrived to live with us all at Broad Street. She was an old-fashioned servant, helping with cooking, cleaning and general clearing up for the six household members. Maggie was wonderful, patient, quiet, respectful of "Mr Bill" as she called him, and a marvellous cook. She was given this room as her own. She always looked out for me, possibly because we both felt on the fringe of this family. Some years later I told her I had used her room when I first arrived at Broad Street and had found it creepy. "Did you hear the footsteps?" she asked. "What footsteps," I said. "Every night," she replied. "They come up to my door, pause and go on again!" "But there is nothing there," I replied. "I know that," she said. "Well, I am sure in the past there must have been more stairs there, going from the space where the suitcases are kept. I have become used to them now." "Are you not tempted to go and have a look?" I asked. "Oh no, I couldn't possibly do that!"

There was a cellar below number 31, its door opening off the dark corridor leading along to Uncle Bill's study and workroom, the stairs directly underneath the main staircase. Whenever I went to his study area, I felt creepy, chilled, and as for the cellar, something unpleasant had happened there, I was sure. We had to go down there to collect the Christmas decoration boxes. I hated it, especially walking down the stairs.

Dear Maggie, she had a heart of gold. Nothing was too much for her. "Maggie, have you seen my book? I have lost it." "What is it called?" "*Marjorie Morningstar*." She paused. "I think Mr Bill has taken it." "Why?" "He perhaps thinks you should not be reading it." Maggie was discreet but I am sure she missed nothing.

This was how it was. A very Victorian attitude to life. I had to behave – I was living in someone else's house and had to fit in with them. My parents expected the best from me and I couldn't let them down. Some of my Ceylon friends, who didn't have relatives in England, or worse still, whose relatives didn't want extra children, expense and responsibility, were sent to paying holiday homes during Christmas and Easter. We heard some terrible stories. Now I feel I was exceedingly lucky to stay in a beautifully run, warm home, with plenty of delicious food, and the bonus of a loving aunt who treated me like her own child. Perhaps I did not appear grateful then, fifty-five years ago.

Chapter 46

Christmas Away From Home

Christmas time came. Uncle Bill rounded us up for the annual holly and ivy gathering. He put his long arm, gloves and secateurs into the back of the station wagon, checked we all had our gloves, scarves and hats, and drove us with his usual care over the hills towards Cheriton. Roo, the dachshund, barked excitedly in the back, anticipating a walk. It was a bright, crisp, cold day, frost still on the wheat stubble, the sun low, streaking the sky red and pink, wind blowing up through the valley. Uncle Bill went shooting most weekends, dressed in his plus fours. He probably had been keeping a lookout for the best place to pick holly, red with berries. We ran around, picking up cut holly stems, broken branches for firewood, dragging them to the car, pulling ivy off the trees, stamping, jumping up and down to keep warm in the freezing wind.

This was to be the first of many Christmas times away from my family.

Returning home in a laden car, throwing off our thick coats and boots, washing our hands, all six of us sat on the sofa and chairs in front of the drawing room fire, having tea while we thawed out. Maggie had rolled in the trolley, heavy with food, and put out the china plates, napkins and ivory-handled tea knives. "Bread and butter first, then

- 160 -

you can have something sweet!" said Aunty Joan. Her cake was always scrumptiously delicious.

The phone call to my parents had been booked to come in just before dinner. Eagerly anticipating talking with them, when the time came the line was indistinct, an echo making conversation impossible. "Happy Christmas, darling. How are you? Is it snowing?" My father's voice down the line reduced me to tears. "Happy Christmas, Daddy. Lovely to hear you!" "What did you say?" "How are you and Mummy?" "Fine – we are missing you." And so it went on. The pips went. "Three minutes is up," said the operator's voice. "Let's have another minute," said my father. He sounded so far away, his voice distant, insubstantial, floating over the airwaves.

I joined in the festivities with a heavy heart, feeling homesick and lonely, despite all Uncle Bill's attempts to cheer me up. He sat at the top of the long, polished wooden table in the dining room. The table was decorated with ivy, crackers, red napkins, crystal wine glasses, cutlery, candles, a glass dish of almonds and raisins, another of silver-covered mandarin oranges and another of walnuts. It looked beautiful. He carved the turkey and we drank a toast to absent friends and family. I tried not to cry.

We pulled crackers, arms linked around the table, put on paper hats, read the jokes, cracked the walnuts, and made boats with half a walnut shell using matchsticks for the masts. Uncle Bill cut a mouth and teeth out of the pith of a whole orange. He squeezed it from the back, making it sick. How he laughed – it was his party trick. The fire glowed deep red beyond the now messy table, filling the room with whiffs of wood smoke which mingled with Uncle Bill's pipe smoke. Glasses clinked, we were replete.

Early next morning, I crept down the thick red-carpeted stairs. The house was still, cold. Wrapped up in my woollen dressing gown, I wrote a long letter to my parents, describing all that we had been doing over Christmas. I imagined them sitting at our dining table. It would be lunch time when my father arrived home with the mail and newspaper. They would be sitting under the fan, the French windows open onto the lush, sun-drenched garden, birds flitting around, Muniandy waiting to serve them lunch. I sighed, looked up, pulled my dressing gown closer and stared out of the playroom window onto a wide, deserted Broad Street. Boxing Day morning. No one around. Frost had whitened the sash window and beyond; all the bare branches of the trees lining the pavement were etched against a grey sky.

I lived for the postman who brought airmail missives: one week from my father, Jocelyn the following. I took them away to my private place, tearing open the blue and red bordered envelopes decorated by brightly coloured rupee stamps. My father was using green ink at this period of his life, writing six carefully numbered, small white airmail sheets in his familiar script. Anecdotes of his daily life, news of Sally, our dog, and his love for me, jumped out from these pages. Touching the smooth paper, closing my eyes, I would feel so close to him. He conveyed more emotion in writing than he ever did when we were together.

Now, many years later, I realise how important these letters were to me. My parents threw me a lifeline. They both had been sent to boarding school, suffering the same searing pangs of homesickness, separation and loneliness. They understood, whereas in England families stayed together, often living close to each other, sharing good and bad times, secure in their togetherness.

My cousins were slowly getting used to this intruder, as I was learning to settle in, to accept them for what they were – generous and as loving as was possible to an angry, defensive child.

Chapter 47

Linch House

Summer arrived, and along with it the news that some of us were going to board at Linch, a big house half a mile from the top of the drive. The school had run out of beds. We were the lucky ones, driven up the school drive every evening. Bouncing around in the school bus, we sang cheerfully, "Mud, mud, glorious mud," making up topical words to fit our mood. We had the sense we were leaving school for a few hours. It was liberating and exciting. Linch House stood on a hill, surrounded with sweet-smelling and gloriously coloured azalea bushes, in a large garden where we were free to roam during the long, warm summer evenings.

Oboe was in charge. She was well-built, rather masculine, and terrifying with her deep voice and Victorian attitudes. But she didn't gather us for illicit prayer groups as the assistant to Apple had tried to do when Apple was not around. That had been decidedly creepy, kneeling on the hard floor of her tiny room, while she touched our heads, suggesting we 'give ourselves to God'.

Oboe had a different way: "You girls don't need to wear brassieres. When I was your age we wrapped a towel around our chests." We tried to keep out of her way when we undressed. We did try to behave. If not, she would shout loudly and bother us.

An extensive walled vegetable and fruit garden was on the left of the driveway. If we arrived a little early we just caught sight of the handsome blonde gardener finishing his work before bicycling home, his shirt casually thrown over his shoulders. One of the senior girls had her eye on him, as well as us. Later in the term she was caught with him behind the sheds in an uncompromising position.

Carefully we watched courgettes and beans growing as the summer days lengthened, fruits ripening under high nets. One warm moon-filled evening, while keeping an eye out for Oboe, we raided the beds. Blackcurrants, redcurrants and raspberries hung full and juicy, quite perfect, ready for picking. We stuffed these exquisite fruits into our mouths, savouring their sharp sweetness, chewing, swallowing handful after handful. I had never tasted such delicacies. Forbidden fruit is so much sweeter. Juice stained our mouths and hands and we giggled together. "Be quiet," hissed Brigit, our lookout. I still remain surprised we were never caught and cannot remember whether Brigit ever got her turn under the nets.

Towards the end of the long summer term Ma B announced in morning prayers: "Girls, I have some exciting news for you all! The school is moving premises. The autumn term will open with the school at West Dean Park. This big house we have leased is close to Chichester. It is about half an hour's drive from here." A stunned silence followed. It was a shock for us all. We were used to this place. We loved the expansive grounds, even though we did have to run around the playing fields every day in preparation for our house sports. Would there be trees we could climb? A swimming pool? I am sure Ma B gave us all the information we wanted; she stressed it would be a huge upheaval for everyone concerned. I was much more excited thinking about my forthcoming summer holidays in Colombo. We still had to compete in Sports Day and swimming sports, write our end-of-term exams, clean our brown wooden desks with bleach and pack our trunks before we were free to go home.

Chapter 48

Alresford

Aunty Joan was a stalwart. Arriving on time at the front door, where our trunks, full and heavy, were lined up, she directed the school handyman to her car. We eased the trunk into her boot, checked I had all my belongings, jumped in, slammed the doors, and were off. Up the drive we went, past the hangar, the rutted top driveway and the lodge, through the gates to freedom. I loved these times my aunt and I had together, not having to share her with my cousins, uncle and her good works. Joan drove carefully along the twisty, narrow lanes, filling me in with family news. "Uncle Bill has a new dog, a springer spaniel which he is training for shooting. We have called him Smudge." So Tigger, a tortoiseshell cat, Roo, a smooth-haired dachshund and Smudge all fought for space on the backdoor mat.

Meals were taken in the family-sized kitchen at the end of a dark corridor leading from the main hall. Originally these were domestic quarters, with a back scullery and small staircase leading up to two rooms, rather dark and gloomy, behind the kitchen. In later life I had many nightmares, often finding myself lost and scared, searching for a person I had forgotten to feed, wandering around corridors and stairs similar to those at Broad Street. My cousin had his model railway laid out up in one of these musty rooms, where girls were not welcome. We cleaned our shoes in the scullery, next to the washing machine. The kitchen was dominated by an Aga, always warm, the source of endless delicious food. On sunny days the kitchen door stood open onto a paved courtyard, allowing sunshine in. Uncle Bill kept his car in the yard; his chickens beyond the barns and greenhouse behind a wrought-iron gate which opened onto his pride and joy, the garden.

This garden was simply beautiful with herbaceous borders along both sides, the old brick walls the perfect backdrop for hollyhocks, flocks, Canterbury bells and delphiniums. A gravel pathway separated these beds and a smooth weed-free green lawn. My cousins and I were bribed: "Five shillings an hour to dig the weeds out of the lawn." We groaned. "Come on now!" It was hard work. Uncle Bill watched us, checking we weren't digging up great dollops of earth with the weeds. He forbade us to bicycle over his lawn but we were allowed to climb the mulberry tree in the middle. We sat up high amongst the leaves and when the tree was in fruit, we gorged ourselves.

Three tall walnut trees stood at the bottom of the garden, next to the compost, quite some distance from the house. Here we gathered with friends to play all sorts of games on the rough grass, sometimes climbing over the flint wall into the empty field.

By now I was sharing my girl cousin's bedroom. We were all much more friendly, taking our turns to help with household chores. Joan would give us a shopping list at breakfast. We walked up the street to the hardware shop – low-ceilinged, dark, full of inviting boxes, screws, bottles, cleaning equipment and crockery – the greengrocer's next door, then around the corner to the chemist, the fish shop, the baker's and butcher's.

'Round the lump' was where we went to walk the dog or just get away. Down the hill we went, chattering, looking through all the windows on our way, the dentist's house, the pottery, past the old flour mill, its wheel now at a standstill. Then along the path beside the watercress beds, which stretched into the distance, lush green leaves standing in clear, flowing water. We turned left onto the narrow tarmac road checking for cars, then left again, back onto a narrow track leading to the ancient, exquisite fulling mill. In earlier centuries this had been used to remove grease from wool fabric, the cloth being mixed with soda or urine. The cloth was the pounded by heavy wooden hammers moved by water rushing through the big wheel. Now this was a pretty cottage straddling the River Itchen, a wooden footbridge parallel with its frontage. We always paused here, leaning on a wooden rail, watching for brown trout in the sparkling water. Moorhens nested in the long reeds by the river bank, willow branches overhung the path.

We turned left again beside the river itself, water weed stretching in green trails along the surface pulled by the flow, making sure the dogs didn't jump in. We could see the sandy bottom: the water was crystal clear. Often a kingfisher was waiting on a branch on the opposite bank. We looked through the arched wooden entrance of an outdoor pool, emptied in winter but now full, where the small, shining white bodies of children splashed and jumped under the sun, shouting with joy at the thrill of cold water fresh from the river.

Chapter 49

Summer Holidays

Finally, the day has arrived. It has been ten long months since I last saw my parents. I feel very different to the girls in my boarding school. Most of them have never been outside England. At weekends and holidays they go home to their families. They haven't experienced heartbreak, separation.

Today I leave for Colombo. I am filled with overwhelming anxiety about flying on my own, mixed with gut-wrenching excitement about going home. Aunty Joan is wonderful, arranging my clothes, helping me to unpack my school trunk and my suitcase, keeping me calm. I've chosen my white blouse, my favourite patterned blue skirt, a cardigan, sandals and a jacket. In my flight bag I have a book, hairbrush, toothpaste and brush and a flannel and spare panties, just in case. We shall be on the plane a long time. It's 1957 and flights take the best part of two days.

We leave after breakfast for Northolt airport. Narrow, twisty roads make it a long drive from Alresford.

"We need to go round the far side of the airfield, to find hut 52." Uncle Bill is driving, his pipe clenched firmly between his teeth. I hate the smell. Sitting in the back, full of suppressed excitement, I look out of the window at fields full of ripening wheat. Soon I shall be looking at palm trees, golden sands, brilliant blue skies. "Are you alright there, Judy?" Aunty Joan turns round, smiles and holds my hand. She knows how I feel. Her childhood was spent travelling back and forth from Ceylon. She too was separated from her parents.

This northern part of the airport is a maze of small huts, with few directions. Uncle Bill is muttering under his breath, reversing the car after several wrong turns. I feel sick, my stomach in a knot. I hope we don't miss the plane. "Here we are. Check you have everything now, Judy." He opens the boot, lifts out my case.

Bright lights glare down on a large group of boys and girls who look as lost as I am feeling. A stewardess checks my ticket and passport. "Wait over there, please. It won't be long before we board." Aunty Joan gives me a hug. "Have a safe journey. Give my love to Daddy."

Suddenly they are gone. I am alone with my bag.

All 120 of us are shepherded onto a bus and driven along the tarmac to a waiting turboprop Britannia, BOAC painted in dark blue on the side. I walk up the metal steps into the aircraft, check my seat number and take my book out of my bag, which is stowed under the seat. I do up my seat belt. I am ready to go.

Engines rev up and the whole plane vibrates. The noise is louder, louder; we start moving, slowly at first, then faster, faster, the nose lifts, and we are off. I let out a sigh, nose squashed against the porthole, looking through clouds at England fading from view.

First stop Frankfurt. We climb off, are issued with a transit card at the door and told, "Do not lose this." We hang around, waiting, looking aimlessly in shop windows, waiting for the announcement to board. Now we are off to Rome. Down the steps again. This is repeated in Beirut, Baghdad, Bahrain. Flying low over the desert into Basra, the dark sky is lit up with flares from oil wells. Here the night air is thick and hot, heavy as a blanket. By now our whole group has relaxed. I have made a few friends, all of us waiting to get home.

We are bussed into Karachi Rest House. It's breakfast time now, after a long, seemingly endless night. A large plate of eggs and bacon is put in front of me. As I cut into my tomato, it squirts all down my white shirt. I look down, mortified, embarrassed. In the Ladies I try to wash off the red stain. I am close to tears.

We take off for Bombay. We are all getting restless. The boys are misbehaving, throwing paper darts at their new friends. Our plane lurches and wobbles as we come in to land through driving rain. It's the monsoon season. Before the aircraft doors are opened, the steward comes through squirting an aerosol can full of foul-smelling spray. I hold my breath, covering my face.

Clutching my transit card I am sitting in the dark cinema watching a film about India. We are delayed, our engines need checking. I hope we will be safe, get there soon. Time drags. I am bored. We sit under the fans on the hard, uncomfortable, sticky seats. It's very hot and airless inside the terminal. I feel crumpled, dirty, tired. There is nothing to do.

It has taken three hours to fix our plane. Now we are off to Colombo, a flight time of another three and a half hours. Time crawls past. Finally, I see the coastline underneath us, the surf breaking on the reef as we approach, our pilot lowering us gently down, our ears popping, the stewardess handing us sweeties. Down, down, I can see the tops of palms, all lined in rows, red earth, scrub, the runway... Whoosh! We have landed at Ratmalana. A cheer goes up.

I brush my hair, tuck in my dirty blouse, put on my sandals. My palms are sweating. I am so excited – we all are. We climb out of our cramped seats and move into the aisle.

The heat hits us as we stand on top of the steps, covering our bodies with warmth. I breathe in the familiar smell. I can't believe we have arrived. Tears of joy prick the backs of my eyes. Down the steps we all clatter, around the plane... and there he is. The familiar figure. His dark hair, dressed in his office whites, waving from crowds of expectant parents.

We all stream across the tarmac, laughing, running the last few steps.

I am enveloped in a bear hug. "Welcome home, darling," says my father.

Acknowledgements

With my love, and thanks, to John who has supported me from start to finish.
Thanks also to Jane Wybrew, Eva Beck and Barbara McNulty for their encouragement